PIANO SAFARI®

REPERTOIRE BOOK 1

BY

KATHERINE FISHER & JULIE KNERR HAGUE

Wendy Lynn Stevens, Contributing Composer

Kelley Shaffer, Cover Artwork

Elisa Lara Campos, Interior Artwork

Visit **pianosafari.com/book1audio2018** and enter the password **18531861k** to download the Audio Tracks for this book.

Copyright © 2018 by Piano Safari, LLC

PIANO SAFARI® REPERTOIRE BOOK 1

TABLE OF CONTENTS

UNIT	TITLE	TYPE	NEW CONCEPT	PAGE
	Table of Contents			2
	Teacher Introduction			6
Intro	Posture	Technique		8
Intro	Piano Hand Shape	Technique		9
Intro	Finger Numbers	Theory	RH, LH, Finger Numbers	10
Intro	Low & High	Theory	Low & High	11
Intro	Rhythm: Note Values and Terms	Theory	♩ ♩ ♫ 𝅝	12
Intro	Alphabet Boogie	Rote	Music Alphabet	15
Intro	Charlie Chipmunk	Rote		16
Intro	March Improvisation	Improvisation		17
Intro	Hungry Herbie Hippo	Rote	Transposition	18
Intro	I Like Bananas	Rote		20
Intro	Outer Space	Rote		22
1	Black Keys	Theory	Black Key Groups	23
1	Ocean Animals	Reading	Repeat Sign	24
1	Tundra Animals	Reading		25
1	Lion Paw	Technique	Arm Weight	26
1	Roaring Lion, Crouching Lion	Improvisation		28

UNIT	TITLE	TYPE	NEW CONCEPT	PAGE
1	King of the African Drum	Rote		30
1	Inchworm	Reading	*Moderato*	32
1	Sam	Reading		33
1	I Love Coffee	Rote		34
1	Old MacDonald Had a Farm	Reading		38
1	Fred the Fish	Reading	$\boldsymbol{p}$ *glissando*	40
1	Swans on the Lake	Rote		42
2	White Keys	Theory		43
2	C D E and F G A B	Theory	White Key Groups	44
2	C D E March	Rote		45
2	Mary Had a Little Lamb	Reading		46
2	F G A B Waltz	Rote		47
2	River Rafting	Reading	*Allegro, ritardando*	48
2	Tall Giraffe	Technique	*Non legato*	50
2	Tall Giraffe and Friends	Improvisation		52
2	A Day in the Life of a Tall Giraffe	Rote		54
2	Fuzzy Wuzzy	Reading	*Andante*	55
2	Ode to Joy	Reading		56
2	Robots	Rote	*Adagio*	58
3	Stave	Theory	Line and Space Notes	60
3	Landmarks	Theory	Treble G and Bass C	62
3	The Interval of a 2nd	Theory	2nds	63

UNIT	TITLE	TYPE	NEW CONCEPT	PAGE
3	My Dog Fritz	Reading	mf 8va	64
3	Creepy Basement	Reading	8vb	65
3	Zechariah Zebra	Technique	Fast Repeated Notes	66
3	Zebra on the Playground	Improvisation		68
3	Zebra on a Pogo Stick	Rote		70
3	City Stroll	Reading		71
3	Chicken Chatter	Reading		72
3	Bingo	Folk		73
3	Dandelion Fluff	Rote		74
3	Kristabel Kangaroo	Reading	♩. 15ma	76
3	Weird Bird	Reading	▬	78
3	Midnight Waltz	Reading	𝄽	79
3	Crocodile in the Nile	Rote		80
3	Thunderstorm Over the Prairie	Improvisation		82
4	The Interval of a 3rd	Theory	3rds	83
4	Skip to My Lou	Rote		84
4	Ferris Wheel	Reading		86
4	Tree Frog	Technique	*Legato* with Bouncy Arm	88
4	Tree Frog in a Rainstorm	Improvisation		90
4	Rainforest Mystery	Rote		92
4	Ping Pong	Reading		94
4	Baa, Baa, Black Sheep	Folk	*D.C. al Fine*	95
4	Autumn	Reading	▬ Phrase Mark	96

UNIT	TITLE	TYPE	NEW CONCEPT	PAGE
4	Kangaroo	Technique	Fast Repeated Notes	98
4	Kangaroo Takes a Trip	Improvisation		100
4	Kristabel Kangaroo Visits Korea	Rote		102
4	Matthew Monkey	Reading		104
4	The Hippopotamus and the Mosquito	Reading	f	105
5	2nds and 3rds	Theory	2nds and 3rds	106
5	Earl the Squirrel	Reading		107
5	Whale in the Deep	Reading	mp	108
5	Soaring Bird	Technique	*Legato* with Smooth Arm	110
5	White Bird, Black Bird	Improvisation		112
5	Hawk on the Mountain Peak	Rote		114
5	Bluebird, Bluebird	Folk		116
5	Twelve Bar Blues	Improvisation		117
5	The Mosquito and the Hippopotamus	Reading		118
5	Dragon Dance	Rote		120
5	A Cowboy's Life	Folk		122
5	Talent Show	Reading	Slurs	124
5	Forest Night	Reading		125
5	Monkey Swinging in a Tree	Technique	Rotation	126
5	Jungle Jumps	Improvisation		128
5	Monkey Blues	Rote		130
	Congratulations			132
	About the Authors			133

PIANO SAFARI® REPERTOIRE BOOK 1

TEACHER INTRODUCTION

Piano Safari® Level 1 consists of:

- Piano Safari® Repertoire Book 1 with Audio Tracks (download code is provided on p. 1)
- Piano Safari® Sight Reading & Rhythm Cards for Book 1
- Piano Safari® Theory Book 1

You may notice that the pieces are at varying levels of difficulty. This was planned for the following reasons:

- To provide appropriate levels of reinforcement
- To provide the challenge and motivation necessary for students to progress
- To generate mental and physical connections between the ears, eyes, fingers, and imagination that come from playing pieces in a variety of textures, types, and levels
- To provide variety in how students learn pieces in order to accommodate different learning modalities

Important Note About Technique: All pieces should be played *non legato* until the introduction of *legato* on p. 88.

Please visit pianosafari.com for the Teacher Guide, Accompaniment Tracks, and for Instructional, Performance, and Reminder Videos.

TYPE OF PIECE	PURPOSE	HOW STUDENTS LEARN THE PIECE
Reading Pieces	• Learn to read music notation • Formally present musical terms and symbols, which students may have already informally encountered in the Rote Pieces	• Read by finger numbers (Units 1 - 2) • Read by intervals of Unisons, 2nds, and 3rds (Units 3 - 5)
Rote Pieces	• Allow students to play more complicated pieces than they can read • Develop aural, technical, musical, rhythmic, and memorisation skills • Develop kinesthetic familiarity with patterns at the piano	• Imitate the teacher • Refer to the score to detect patterns • Reminder Videos for home practice • Audio Tracks for musical understanding. Pieces with Audio Tracks are denoted by the following symbol:
Technical Exercises	• Master basic motions of beginning piano technique	• Imitate the teacher • Refer to the score to detect patterns • Reminder Videos for home practice • Audio Tracks for musical understanding
Improvisation Pieces	• Develop creativity • Use technical motions creatively	• Imitate the teacher • Explore sounds on the piano
Folk Songs	• Allow students to play melodies they recognise • Practise finger numbers beyond the pre-stave portion of study	• Read by finger numbers and intervals • Audio Tracks for musical understanding
Sight Reading & Rhythm Cards for Book 1	• Reinforce reading skills • Reinforce rhythmic skills	• Read by finger numbers (Levels A - B) • Read by intervals on the stave, beginning on Landmark Notes, using Unisons, 2nds, and 3rds (Levels C - E)

POSTURE

INTRODUCTION
TECHNIQUE

PROPER POSTURE

Bench Position

Sit on the front half of the bench. Place your feet on a foot stool or pedal extender if you cannot reach the floor.

Distance

Check your distance from the piano by putting your arms straight out, making fists with your hands, and touching the fallboard. You should be able to reach it without leaning forward or backward.

Height

Check your height by placing your hands gently on the keys. Forearms should be level with the keyboard.

Head and Shoulders

Your head should be balanced on top of the spine with your shoulders relaxed.

WHAT DO YOU THINK?

Discuss with your teacher how Isaiah's posture looks in this picture. What does he need to change?

You be the teacher! Have your teacher sit at the piano. Tell your teacher what is good posture and what needs to be fixed.

Take a picture or a video of yourself at home to check your posture.

PIANO HAND SHAPE

INTRODUCTION
TECHNIQUE

Check

Check your own piano hand shape!

Bridge ☐

Wrist ☐

Fingers ☐

Finger Nail Joints ☐

Finger 1 ☐

Finger 5 ☐

PROPER PIANO HAND SHAPE

- The hand is in a gently curved position with the bridge slightly raised.

- The wrist is level with the arm.

- The fingers maintain a natural curve as they are when hanging by the side of your body. The finger nail joints are firm.

- Fingers 1 and 5 rest on the outer corners, as shown in the pictures above.

FINGER NUMBERS

INTRODUCTION
THEORY

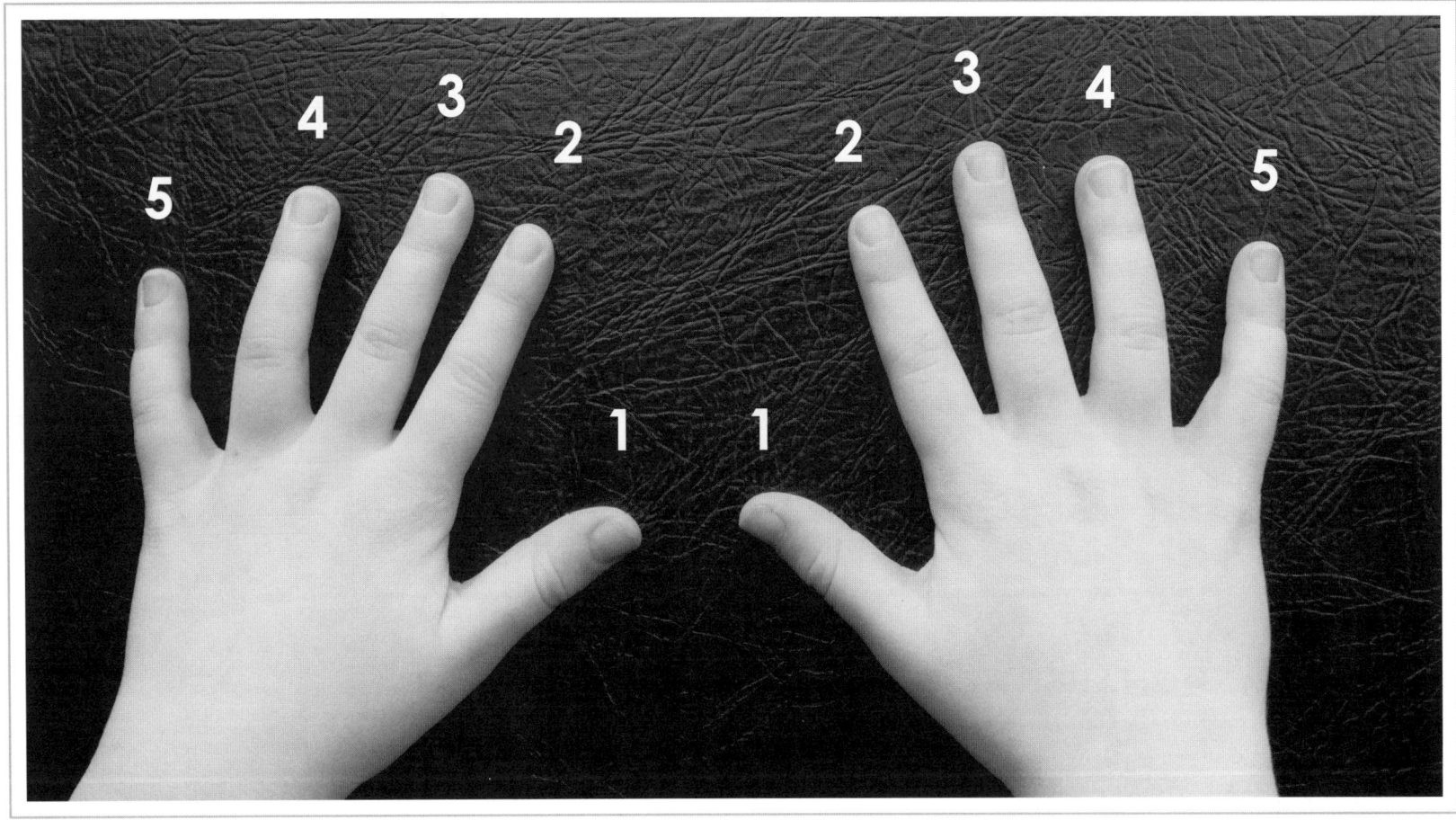

Tap each finger gently four times on the fallboard while saying the finger numbers.

LOW & HIGH

INTRODUCTION
THEORY

Lions make **Low** sounds.

Low sounds are on the **Left** side of the keyboard.

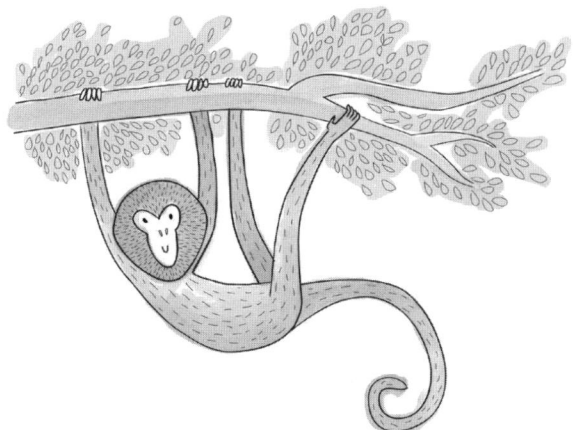

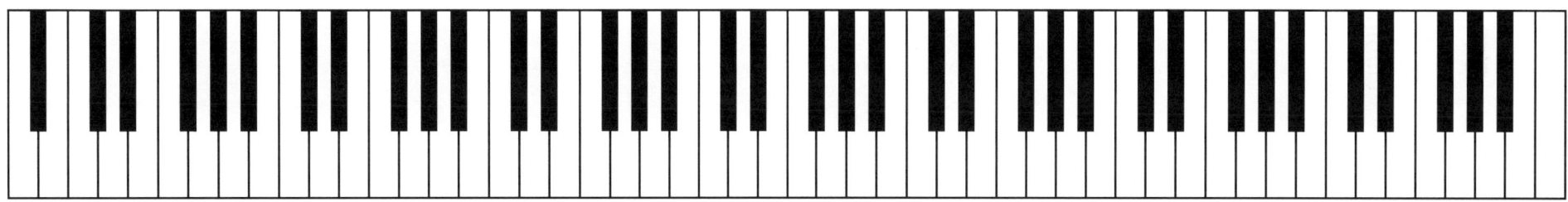

Play

- Low animal sounds
- High animal sounds

Monkeys make **High** sounds.

High sounds are on the **Right** side of the keyboard.

11

RHYTHM
Note Values

INTRODUCTION
THEORY

Crotchet
1 beat

Say "Ta" when counting Crotchets.

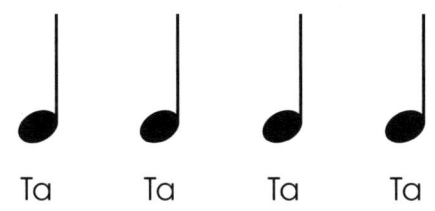

Ta   Ta   Ta   Ta

Draw Crotchets in the boxes.

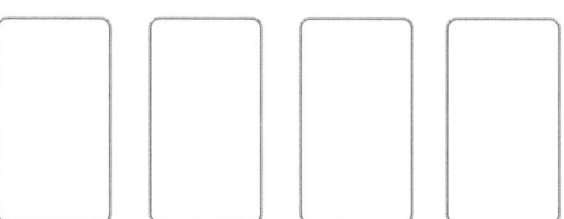

Quavers
Two Quavers = 1 beat

Say "Ta - ti" when counting Quavers.

Ta - ti   Ta - ti   Ta - ti   Ta - ti

Draw Quavers in the boxes.

Four Quavers
Four Quavers = 2 beats

Quavers may also be barred in groups of four.

Ta - ti   Ta - ti   Ta - ti   Ta - ti

Draw four Quavers in the box.

Minim
2 beats

Say "Ta - 2" when counting Minims.

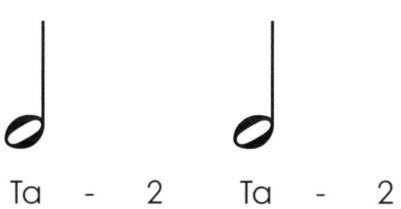

Ta - 2   Ta - 2

Draw Minims in the boxes.

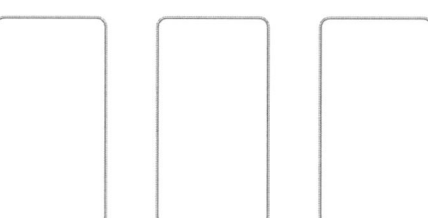

Semibreve
4 beats

Say "Ta - 2 - 3 - 4" when counting Semibreves.

Ta - 2 - 3 - 4

Draw Semibreves in the boxes.

RHYTHM
Terms

INTRODUCTION
THEORY

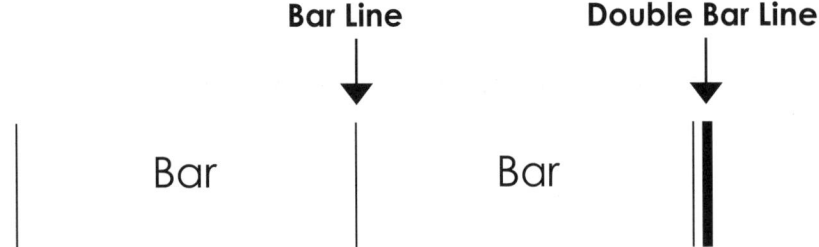

- A **Bar Line** divides notes into groups.
- A **Bar** is the distance between each Bar Line.
- A **Double Bar Line** signals the end of the piece.

Tap

- Trace the bar lines with your favorite colour. Circle the double bar line.
- Tap and count the rhythm.

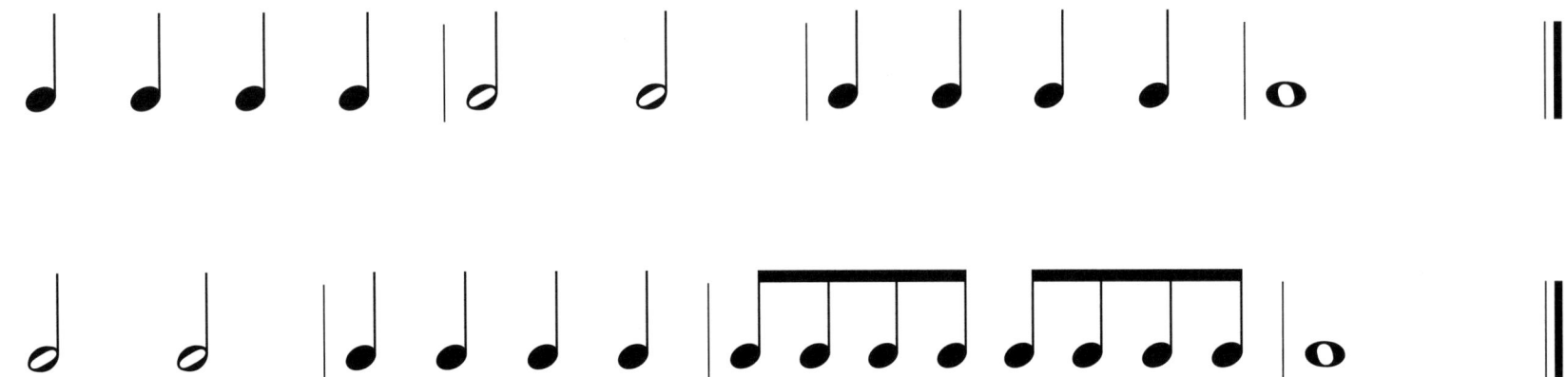

ALPHABET BOOGIE

INTRODUCTION
ROTE

Energetically

Hague & C. Fisher

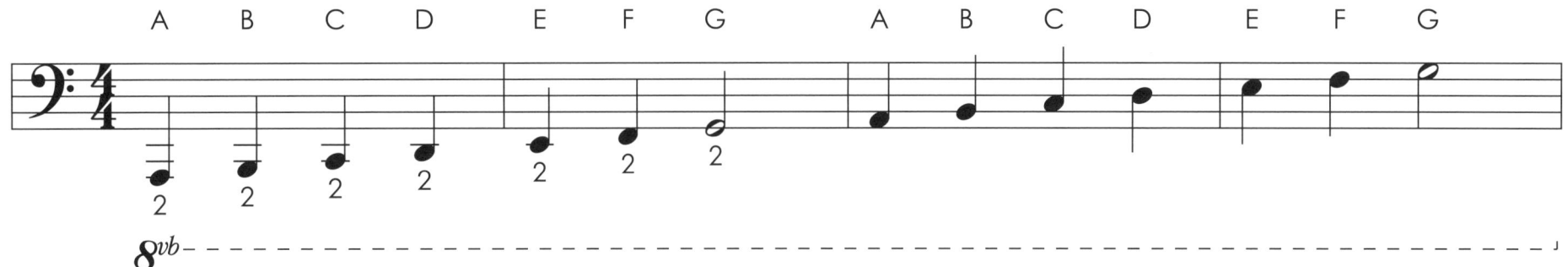

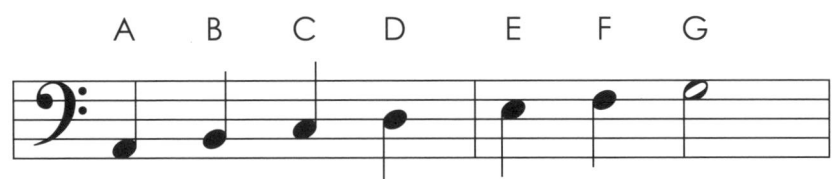

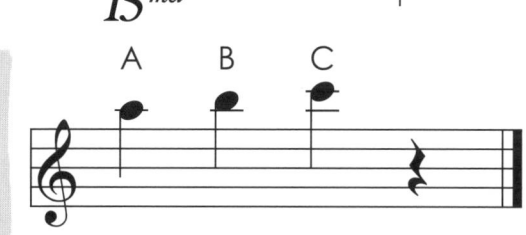

Continue playing every key to the top of the piano.

Check off when mastered.

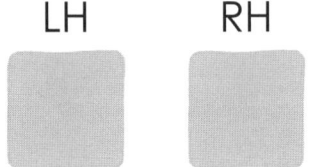

Teacher Accompaniment. Student plays as written.

Repeat 4 times.

CHARLIE CHIPMUNK

Hague

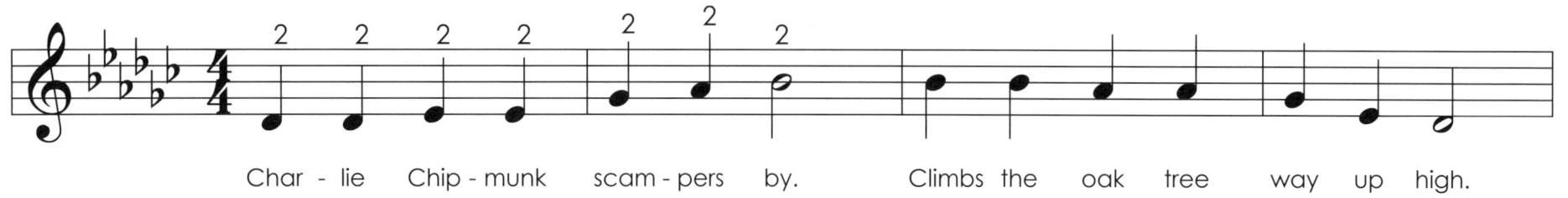

Char - lie Chip - munk scam - pers by. Climbs the oak tree way up high.

Cros - ses bran - ches on the run. Chip - munk life is so much fun!

Check off when mastered.

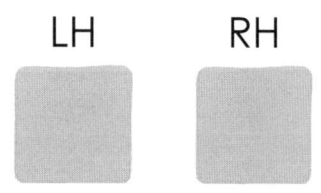

Teacher Accompaniment

MARCH IMPROVISATION

INTRODUCTION
IMPROVISATION

Student Part: Improvise a march on the black keys.

Teacher Part:

Hague

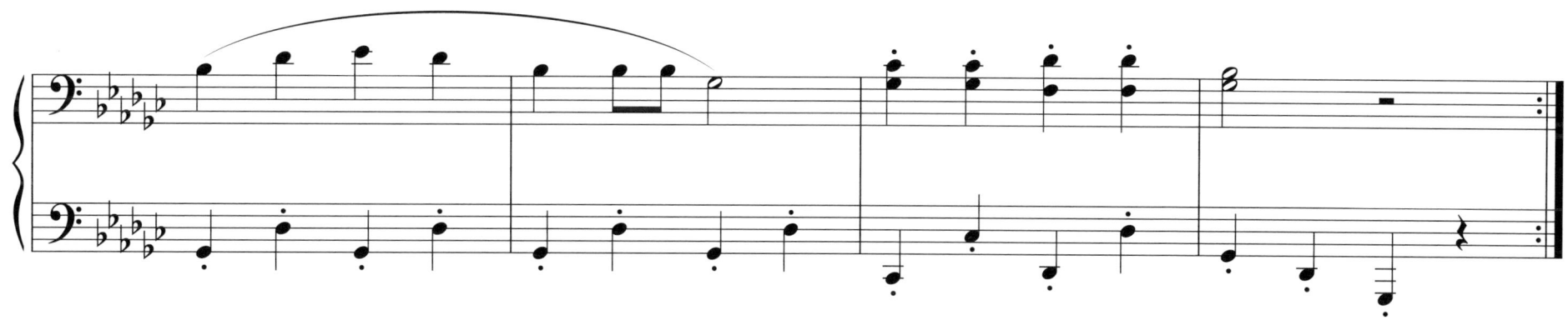

HUNGRY HERBIE HIPPO

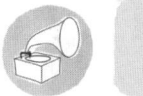
INTRODUCTION
ROTE

Traditional, arr. Hague

Her - bie Hip - po eats his leaves, and Her - bie Hip - po likes his grass. But

Her - bie Hip - po - pot - a - mus, he real - ly wants a cheese - bur - ger.

Check off when mastered.

Black Keys

Teacher Accompaniment

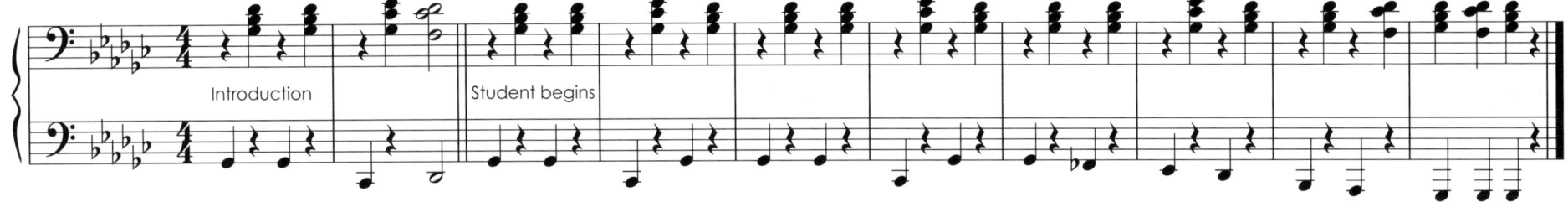

Play **Hungry Herbie Hippo** in the following keys.

Skip the penny note (A♯) and end on the dime note (B).

 B

Skip the penny notes.

 C

Skip the penny notes.

 F

Skip the penny notes.

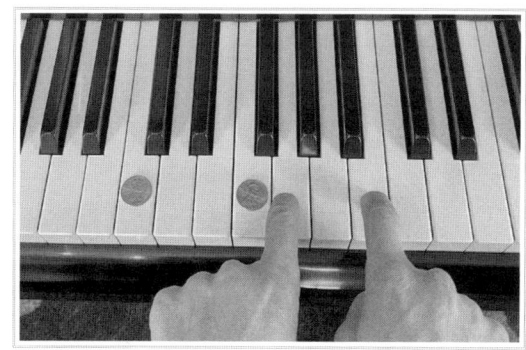 G

Teacher Accompaniments for the transpositions are available at pianosafari.com under Resources.

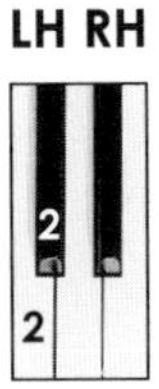

I LIKE BANANAS

 INTRODUCTION ROTE

Hague

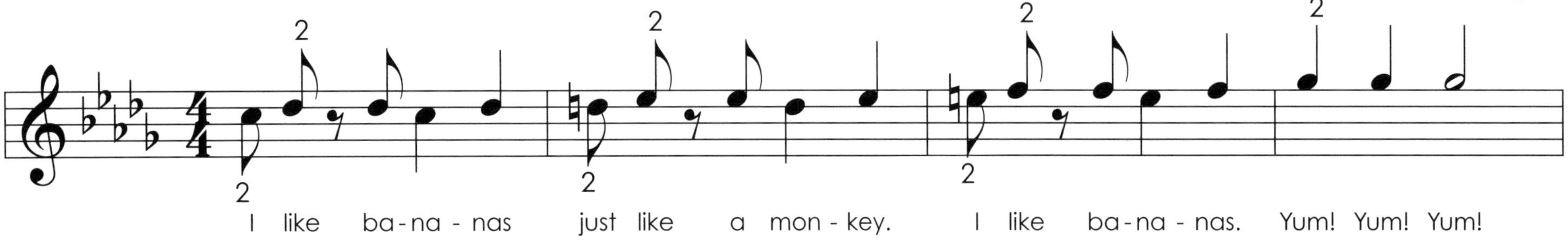

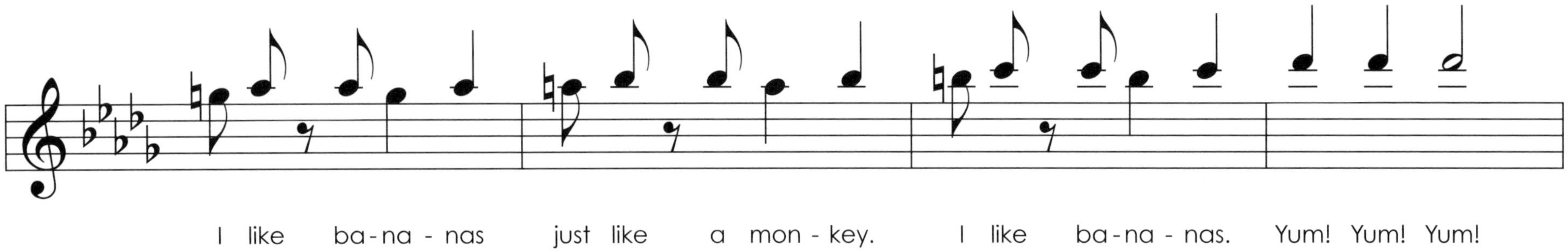

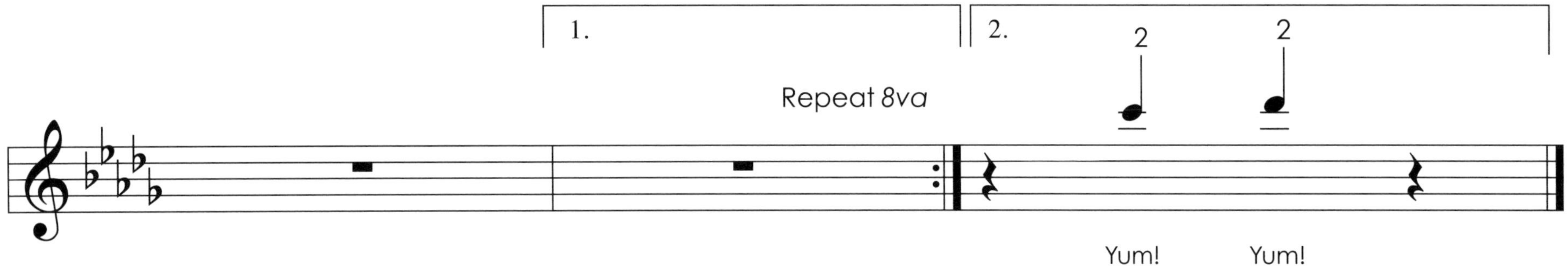

I like ba-na-nas just like a mon-key. I like ba-na-nas. Yum! Yum! Yum!

I like ba-na-nas just like a mon-key. I like ba-na-nas. Yum! Yum! Yum!

1.
Repeat 8va

2.
Yum! Yum!

Teacher Accompaniment

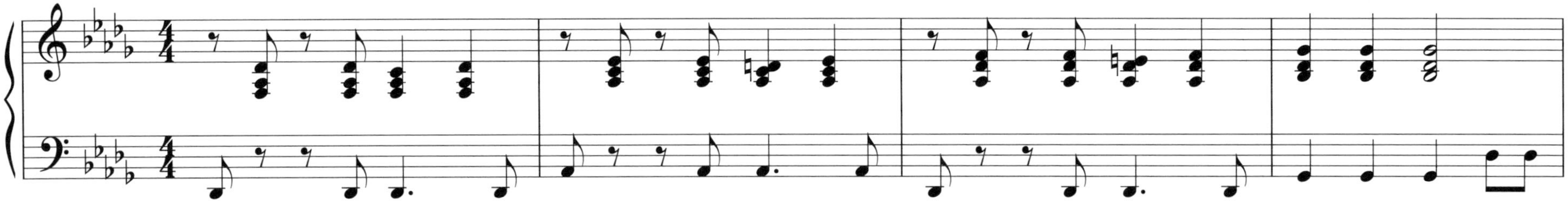

On the repeat, choose a different food and animal.

I like _____ just like a _____.
　　　　　food　　　　　　　　animal

Potatoes　　　　　Burritos　　　　　Zucchini　　　　　Spaghetti

Turtle　　　　　Panda　　　　　Puppy　　　　　Tiger

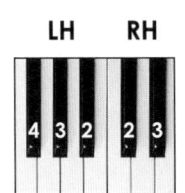

OUTER SPACE

 INTRODUCTION ROTE

Hague

Draw something from outer space and improvise music for it.

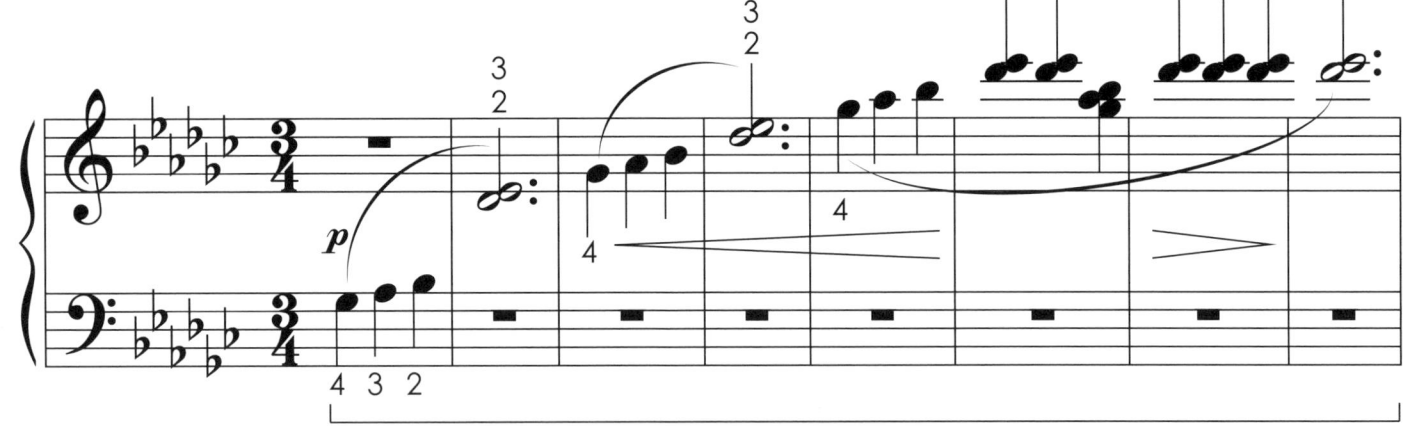

Another space object

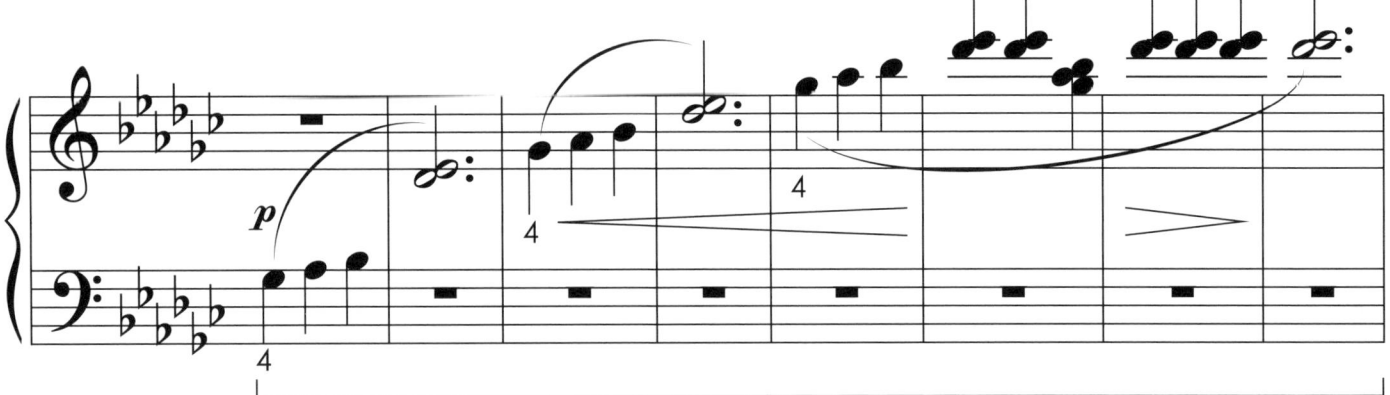

Shooting Star *glissando* on black keys

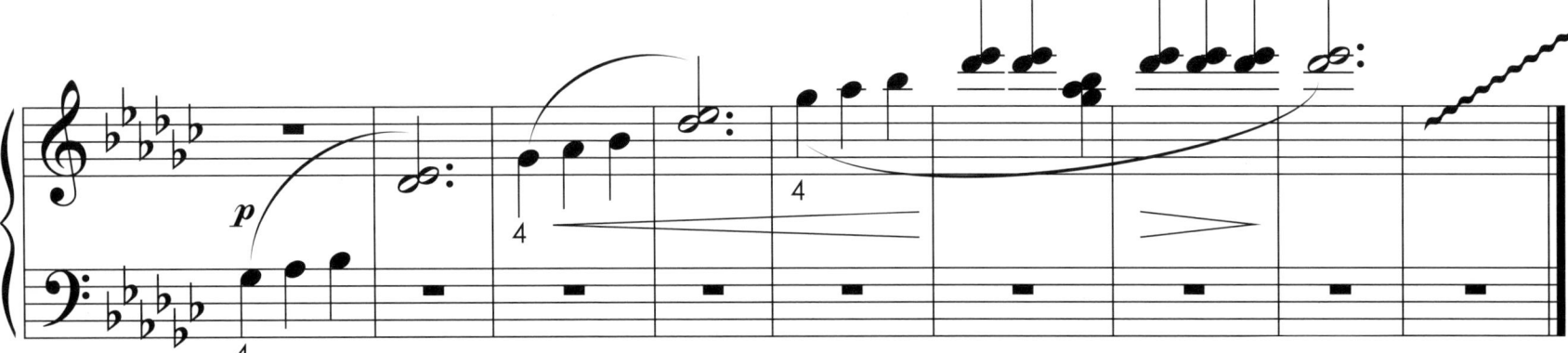

BLACK KEYS

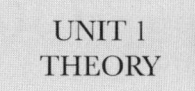

UNIT 1
THEORY

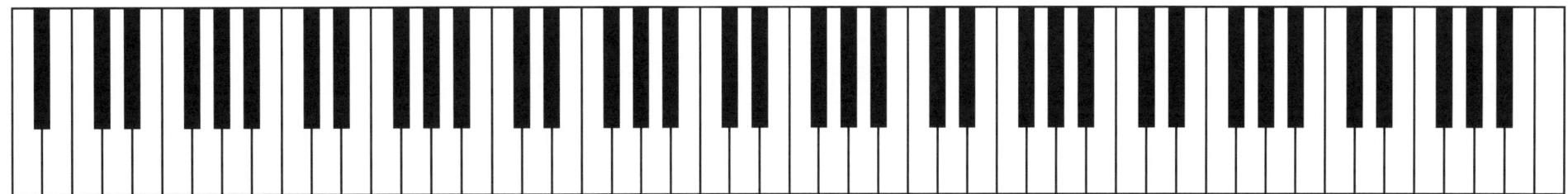

On the keyboard above:

Circle the groups of 2 black keys with green.

Draw a square around the groups of 3 black keys with orange.

Draw a triangle around the leftover 1 black key with purple.

Draw a monkey on the high part of the keyboard.

Draw a lion on the low part of the keyboard.

On your piano:

How many groups of 2 black keys are there? _____

How many groups of 3 black keys are there? _____

Challenge:

How many black keys are there? _____

How many white keys are there? _____

How many keys are there altogether? _____

Assign **Piano Safari Sight Reading & Rhythm Cards Level A** during Unit 1.

OCEAN ANIMALS

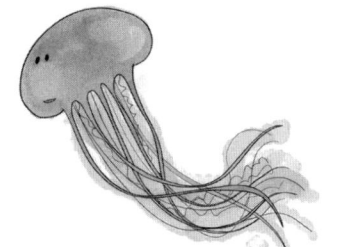

UNIT 1
READING

Hague

Oc - to - pus, Oc - to - pus, Mad - am Oc - to - pus.
Man - a - tee, Man - a - tee, Mis - ter Man - a - tee.
Jel - ly - fish, Jel - ly - fish, Mis - sus Jel - ly - fish.

Stick - y, slim - y, ink - y, grim - y. Mad - am Oc - to - pus.
Full of blub - ber, feels like rub - ber. Mis - ter Man - a - tee.
Soft and mush - y, warm and gush - y. Mis - sus Jel - ly - fish.

𝄇 is a **Repeat Sign**. It means to play again from the beginning.

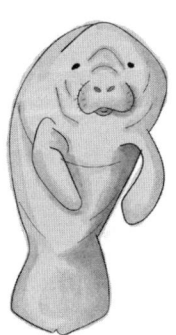

Teacher Accompaniment. Student begins on the G♭ above Middle C. Repeat for each verse.

24

TUNDRA ANIMALS

UNIT 1
READING

Hague & Fisher

Mad - am	Car - i - bou	finds	green	moss	to	chew.
Mis - sus	Arc - tic Fox	lives	a -	mong	the	rocks.
Mis - ter	Po - lar Bear	roams	through	frig -	id	air.

Ant - lers high,	herd near - by.	Mad - am	Car - i - bou.
Bush - y tail	blocks the gale.	Mis - sus	Arc - tic Fox.
Find - ing fish	is his wish.	Mis - ter	Po - lar Bear.

Teacher Accompaniment. Student begins on the B♭ below Middle C. Repeat for each verse.

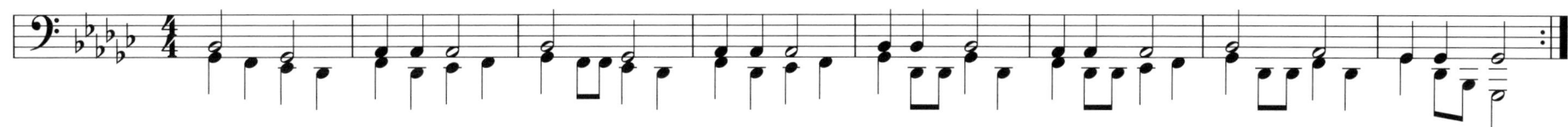

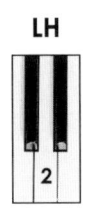

LION PAW
Left Hand

UNIT 1
TECHNIQUE

Hague

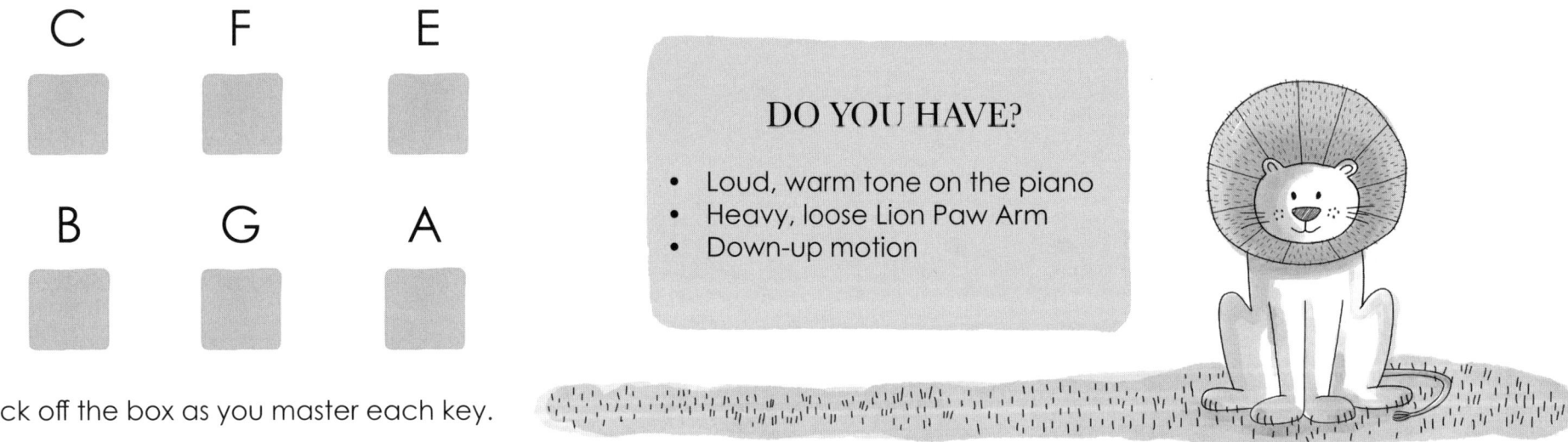

After practising Lion Paw on D, play on other white keys.

| C | F | E |
| B | G | A |

DO YOU HAVE?

- Loud, warm tone on the piano
- Heavy, loose Lion Paw Arm
- Down-up motion

Check off the box as you master each key.

Teacher Accompaniment. Transpose for other white keys.

LION PAW
Right Hand

UNIT 1
TECHNIQUE

Hague

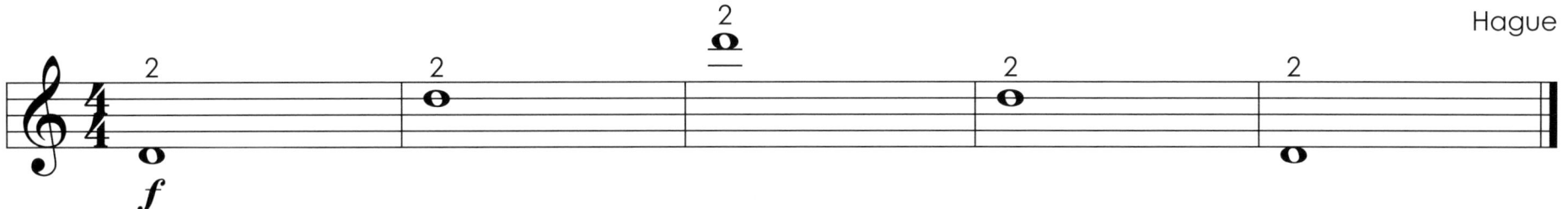

After practising Lion Paw on D, play on other white keys.

C   F   E   B   G   A

Check off the box as you master each key.

Teacher Accompaniment. Transpose for other white keys.

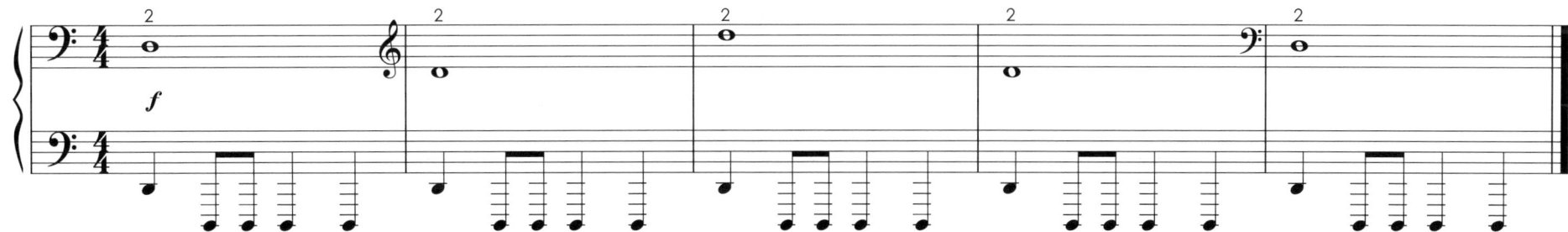

ROARING LION, CROUCHING LION

UNIT 1
IMPROVISATION

Step 1 — Learn the three Lion Patterns.

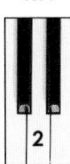

1. Roaring Lion

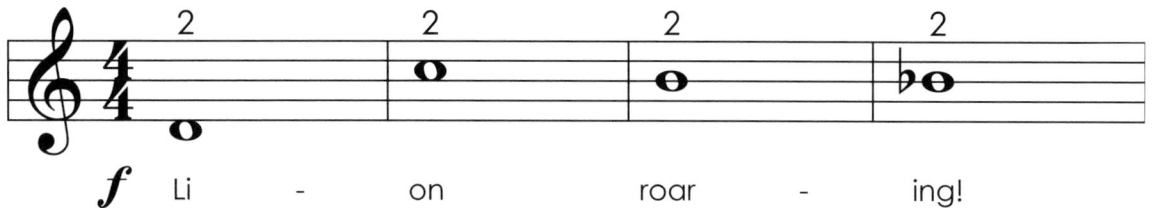

f Li - on roar - ing!

2. Crouching Lion

mp Crouch - ing in the grass.

3. Your Lion — Play Lion Paw Drops on any white key.

Teacher Accompaniment

Repeat for each Lion Pattern.

Hague

Step 2

After learning the Lion Patterns, play them in the order below while your teacher plays the accompaniment.

| Roaring | Roaring | Crouching | Roaring |

| Your Lion | Your Lion | Your Lion | Roaring |

Step 3

Download the Roaring Lion, Crouching Lion Cards from pianosafari.com under Resources.
Create your own piece by putting the cards in the order of your choosing.

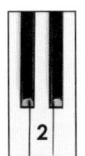

KING OF THE AFRICAN DRUM

UNIT 1
ROTE

Ferociously

Hague

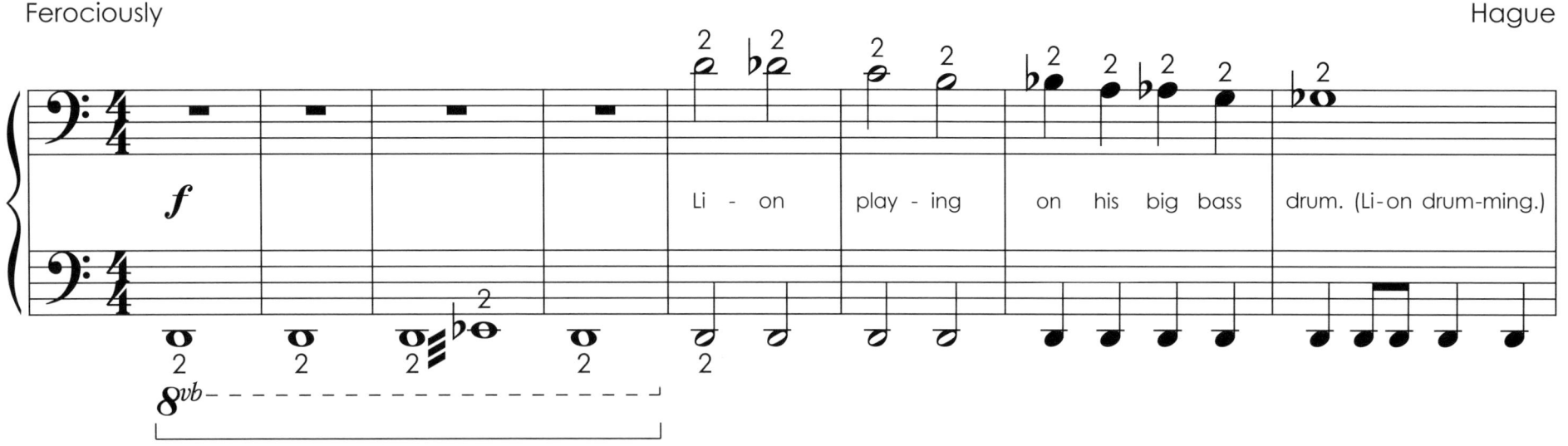

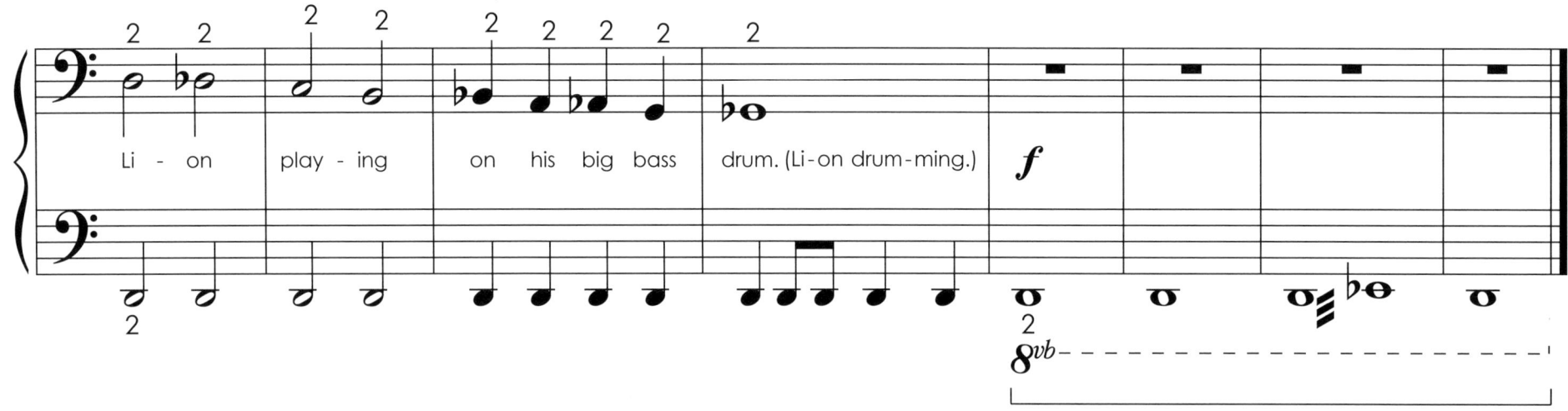

The pictures below show the form of this piece.

- The low part that sounds like a drum comes first.

- The lion theme comes next.

- The lion theme repeats an octave lower.

- The piece ends with the low drum part.

INCHWORM

UNIT 1 READING

Hague

Moderato is the Italian word for playing at a moderate tempo.

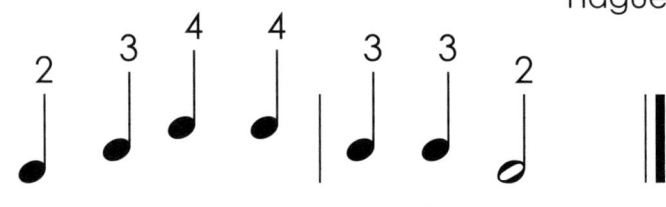
How's your day been? What is new?

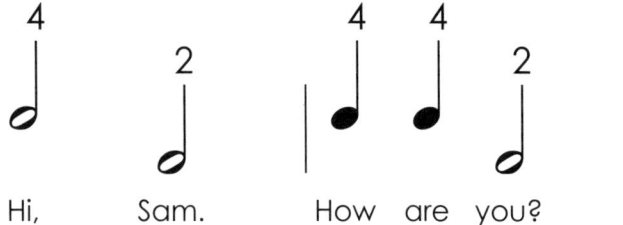
Hi, Sam. How are you?

Move up an octave for each group.

Out to vis - it my friend, Sam.

Moderato

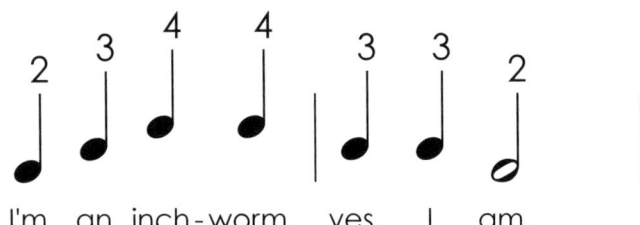
I'm an inch - worm, yes, I am.

Teacher Accompaniment. Swing quavers. Student begins on the G♭ above Middle C.

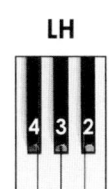

SAM

UNIT 1
READING

Moderato

Hague

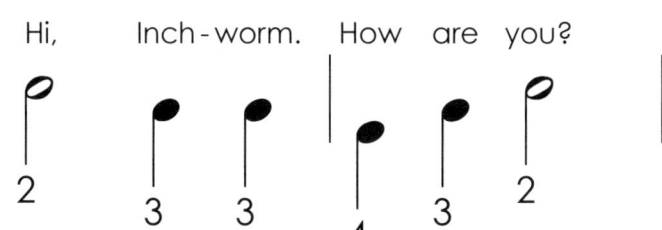

Move down an octave for each group.

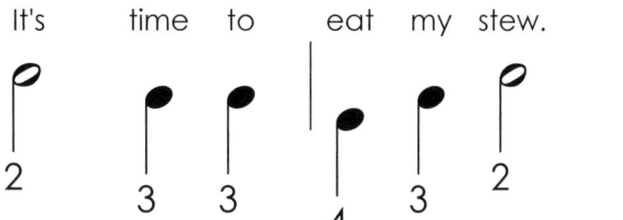

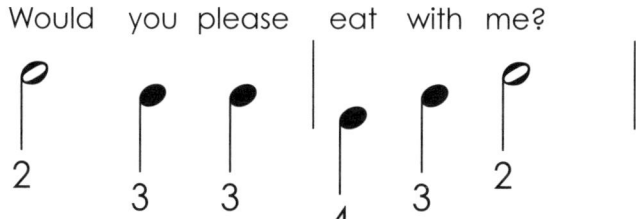

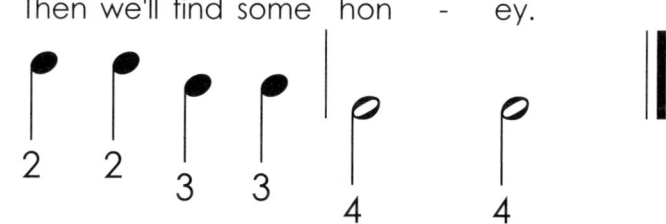

Teacher Accompaniment. Swing quavers. Student begins on the B♭ above Middle C.

I LOVE COFFEE

UNIT 1
ROTE

Part 1

Traditional, arr. Bernard & Carolyn Shaak

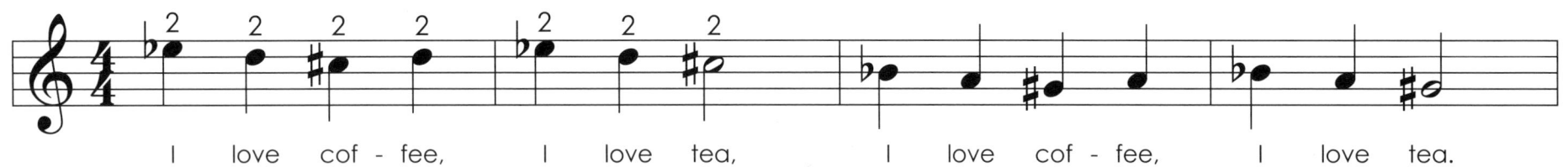

I love cof - fee, I love tea, I love cof - fee, I love tea.

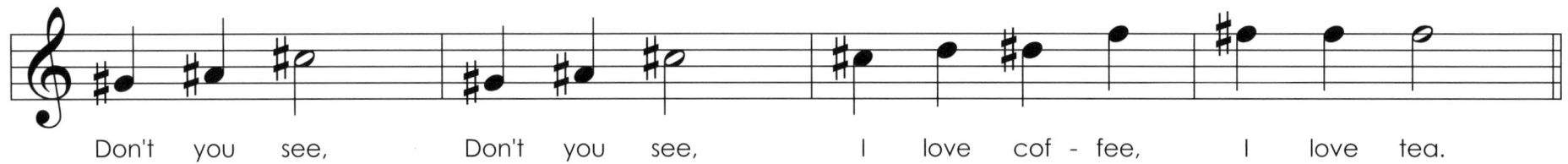

Don't you see, Don't you see, I love cof - fee, I love tea.

Teacher Accompaniment

Copyright © 1978 by Bernard & Carolyn Shaak, www.shaakpianomusic.com. Used with permission.

Part 4

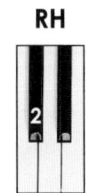
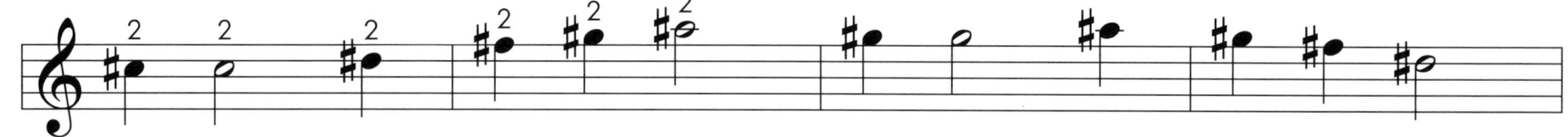

Part 5

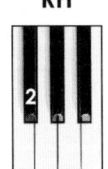
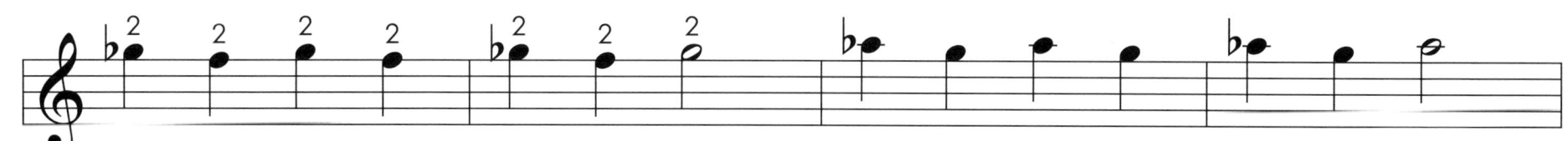

Part 6

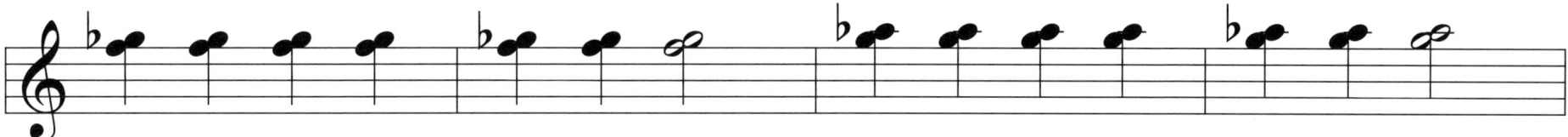

Ending

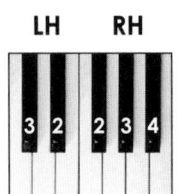

LH
RH
3 2 2 3 4

OLD MACDONALD HAD A FARM

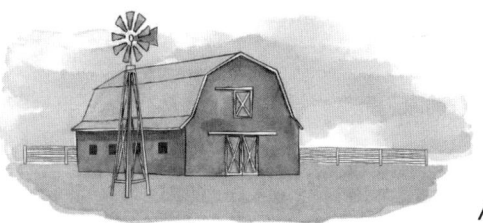

UNIT 1
READING

American Folk Song, arr. Joey Lieber

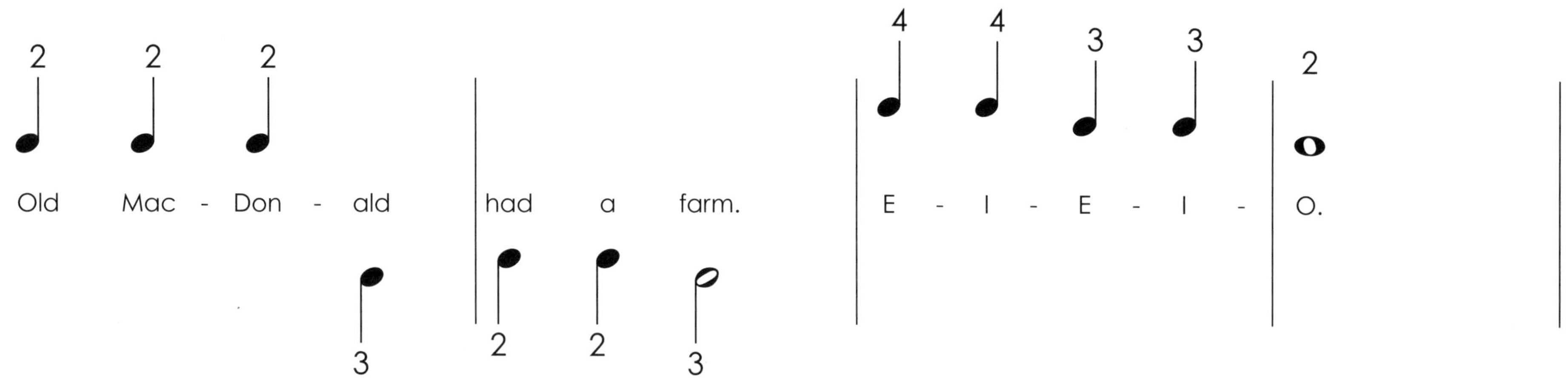

Old Mac - Don - ald had a farm.
E - I - E - I - O.

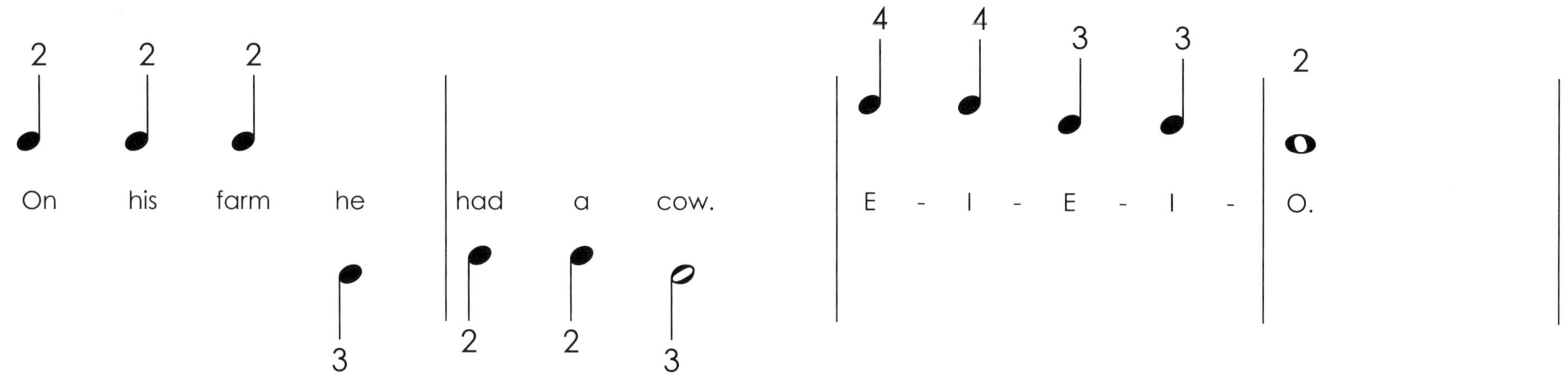

On his farm he had a cow.
E - I - E - I - O.

Teacher Accompaniment. Swing quavers. Student plays on the black keys an octave above Middle C.

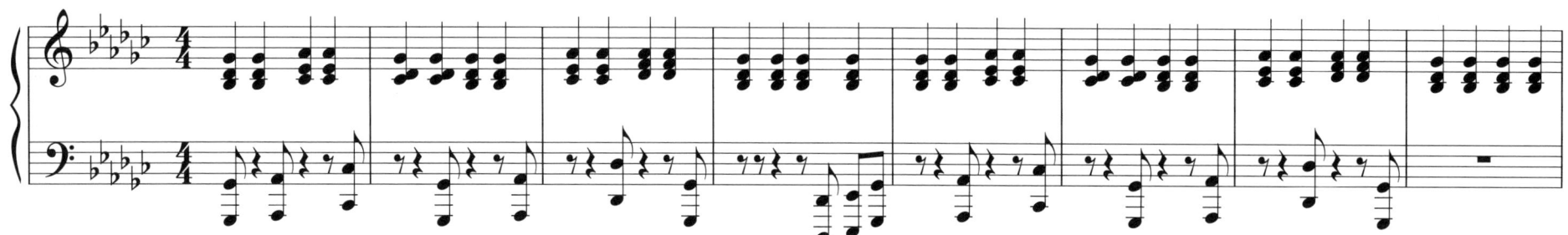

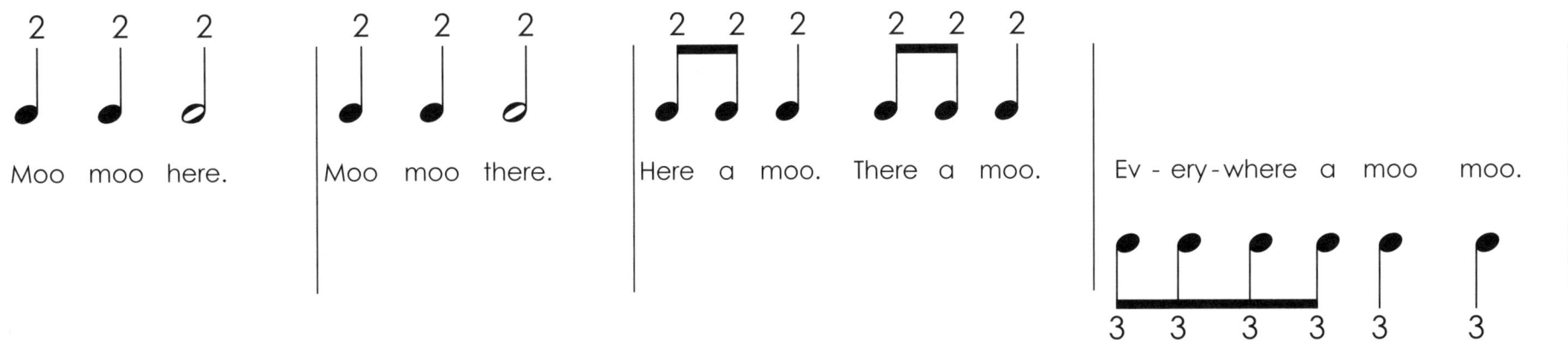
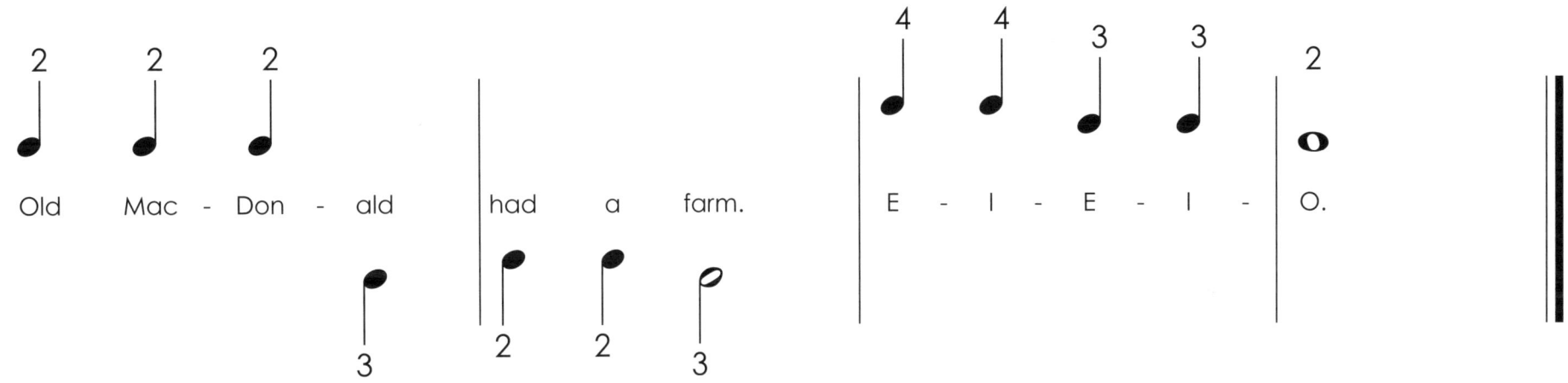
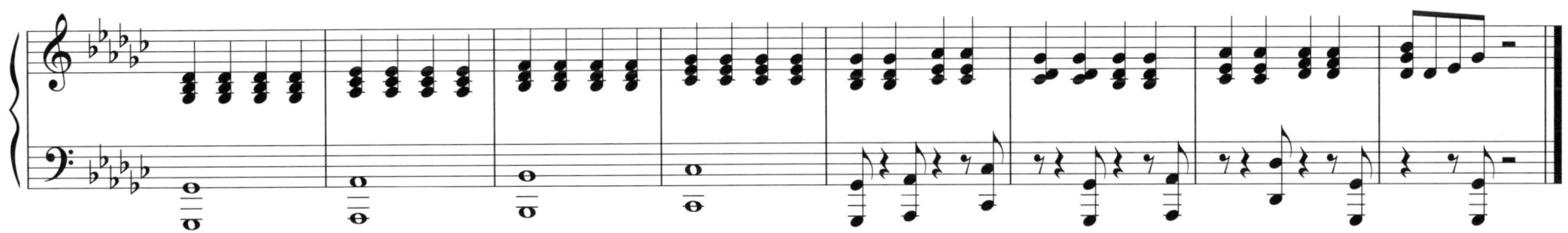

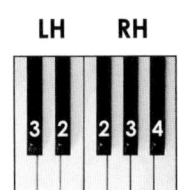

FRED THE FISH

UNIT 1 READING

Hague

Draw Fred.
Improvise fish music
on the black keys.

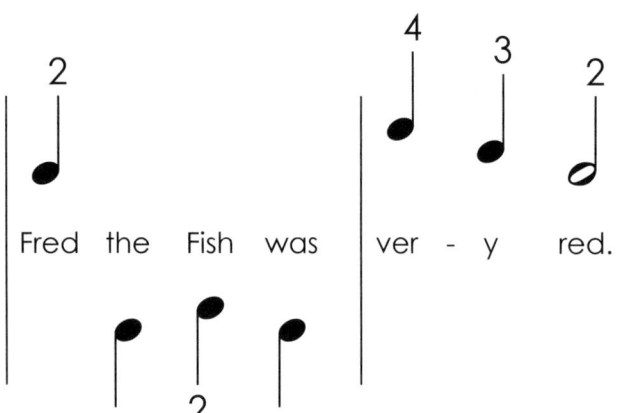

Once there was a | fish named Fred. | Fred the Fish was | ver - y red.

Draw a bird.
Improvise bird music
high on the black keys.

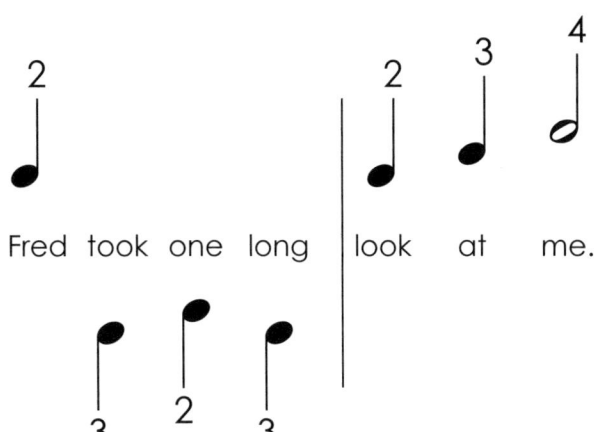
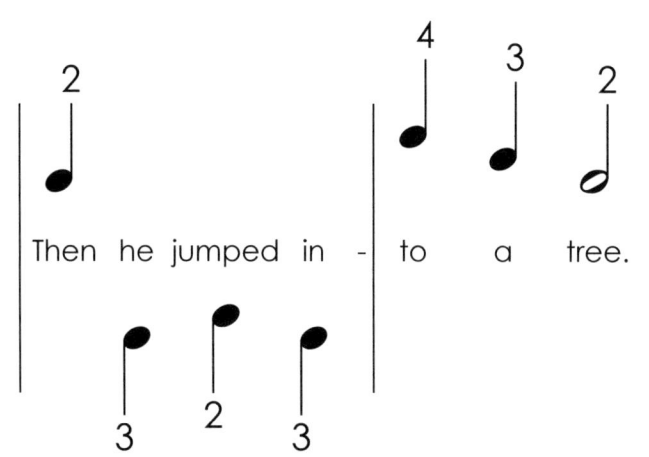

Fred took one long | look at me. | Then he jumped in - to a tree.

Teacher Accompaniment. Student plays on the black keys an octave above Middle C.

Repeat 4x:
- First line
- Fish improvisation
- Second line
- Bird improvisation

40

p *piano* means to play quietly by depressing the keys gently and slowly.

A *glissando* is played by dragging the hand along the keys. Use the black keys for this *glissando*.

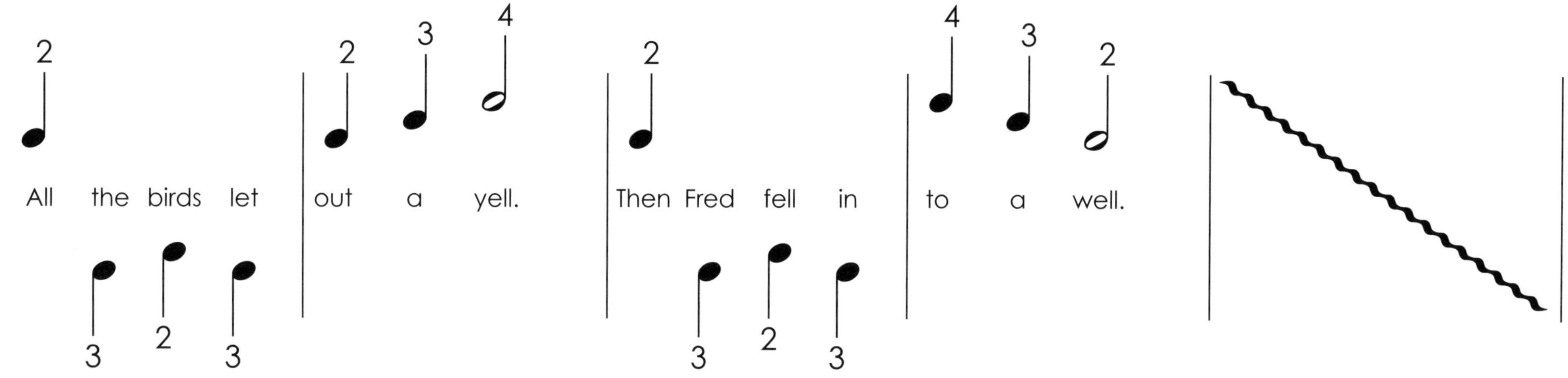

All the birds let | out a yell. | Then Fred fell in | to a well.

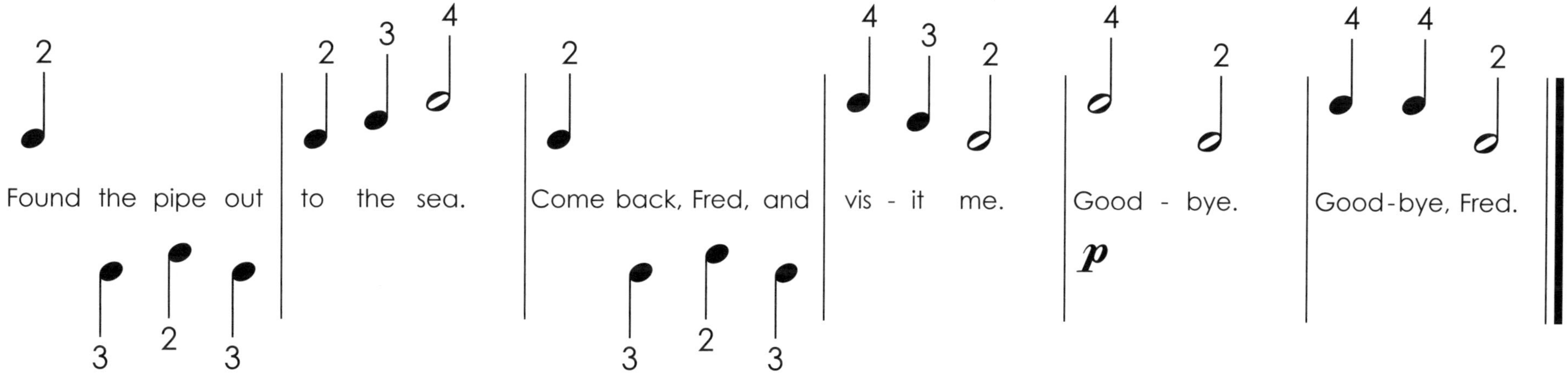

Found the pipe out | to the sea. | Come back, Fred, and | vis - it me. | Good - bye. ***p*** | Good-bye, Fred.

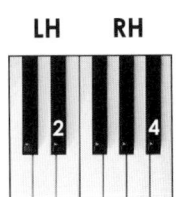

SWANS ON THE LAKE

UNIT 1
ROTE

Gently

Hague

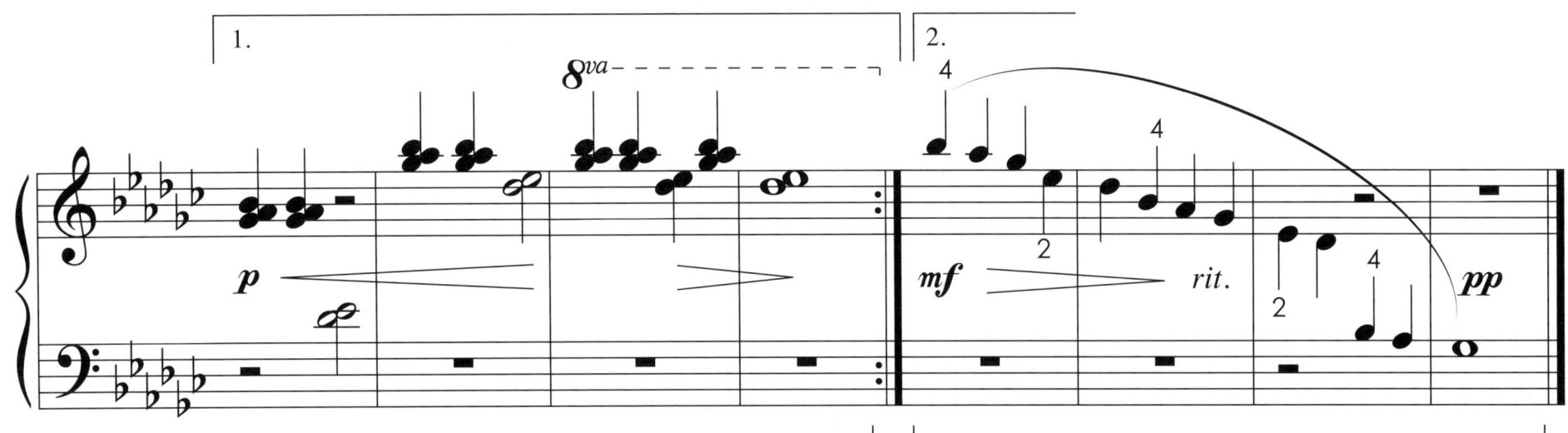

WHITE KEYS

UNIT 2
THEORY

The white keys on the piano move up in order of the alphabet from the letter **A** through the letter **G**:

A B C D E F G

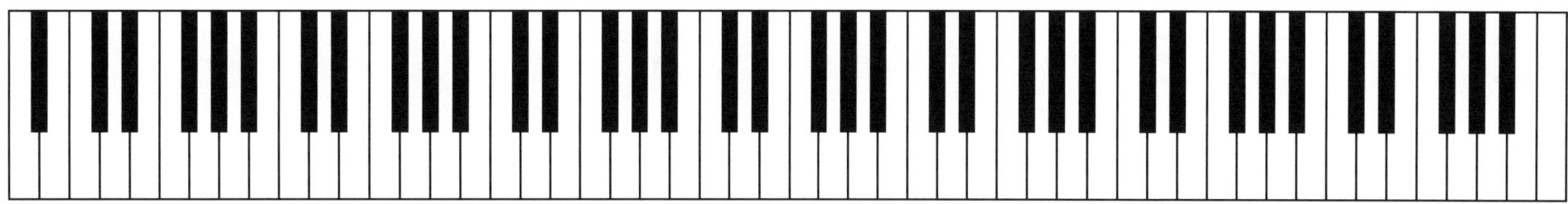

The lowest note on the piano is **A**.

The highest note on the piano is **C**.

Write

Write the Musical Alphabet: ____ ____ ____ ____ ____ ____ ____

Now write it backwards: ____ ____ ____ ____ ____ ____ ____

Play

Practise the Musical Alphabet by playing Alphabet Boogie (p. 15).

Assign **Piano Safari Sight Reading & Rhythm Cards Level B** during Unit 2.

C D E

Write

Write the correct letter name on each key.

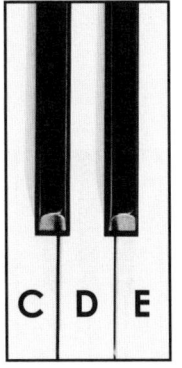 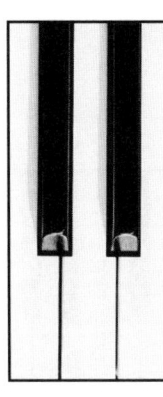 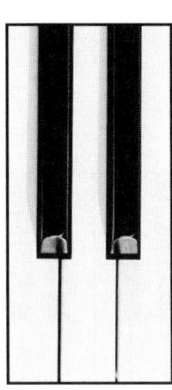 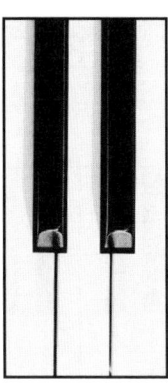

The white keys that surround the group of two black keys are **C D E**.

Play

On your piano:

- Play the **C D E** groups with your RH.
- Play the **C D E** groups with your LH.
- Play every **C**.
- Play every **D**.
- Play every **E**.

F G A B

Write

Write the correct letter name on each key.

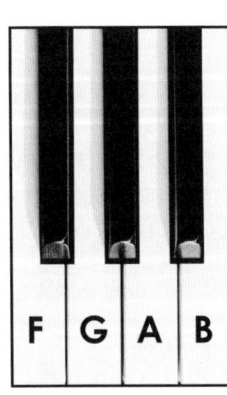 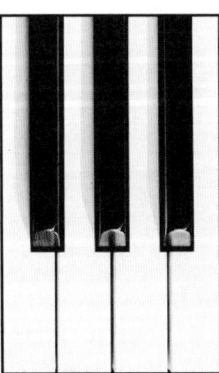 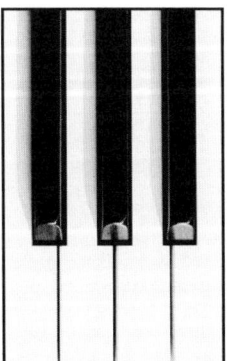 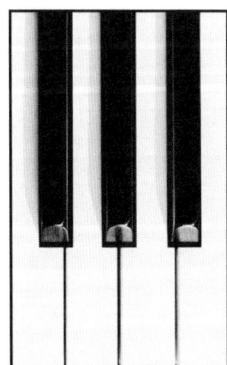

The white keys that surround the group of three black keys are **F G A B**.

Play

On your piano:

- Play the **F G A B** groups with your RH.
- Play the **F G A B** groups with your LH.
- Play every **F**.
- Play every **G**.
- Play every **A**.
- Play every **B**.

C D E MARCH

Marching

Hague

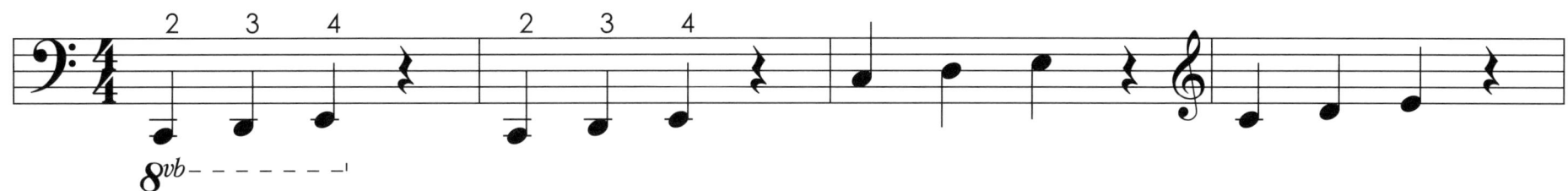

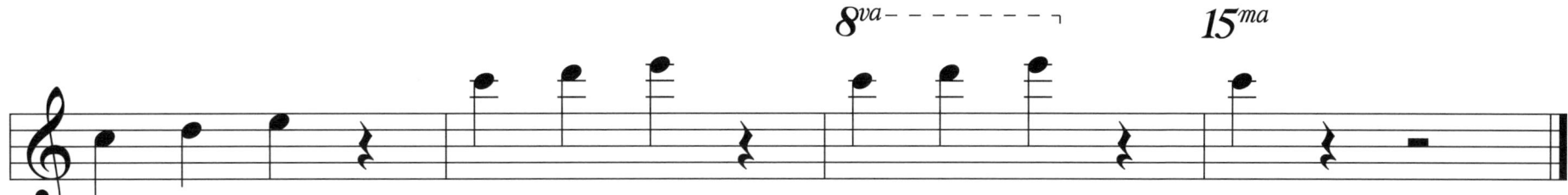

Check off when mastered.

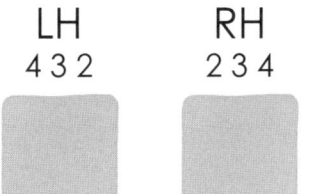

Teacher Accompaniment

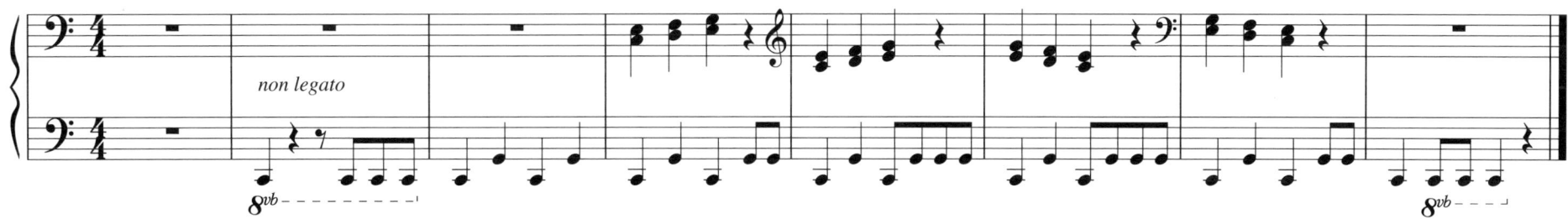

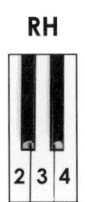

MARY HAD A LITTLE LAMB

UNIT 2
READING

Traditional, arr. Christopher Fisher

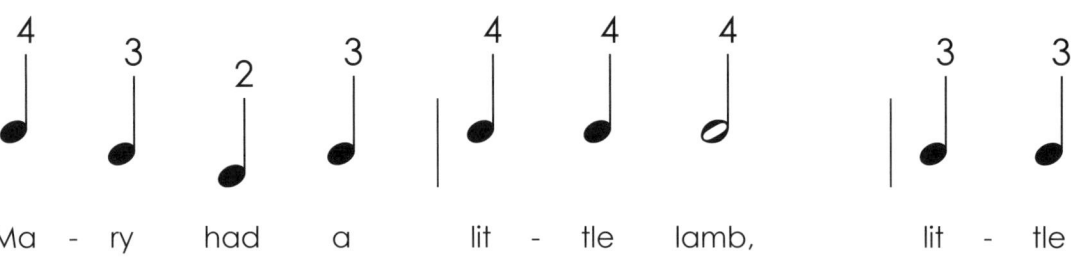

Ma - ry had a lit - tle lamb, lit - tle lamb, lit - tle lamb.

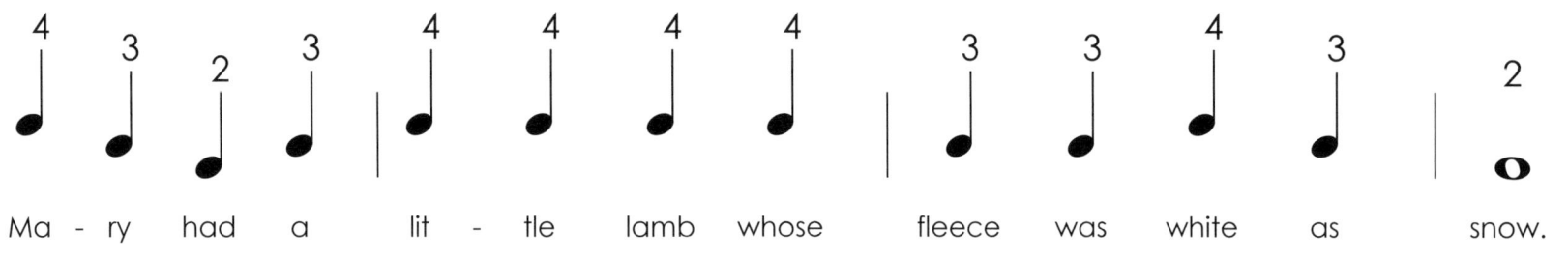

Ma - ry had a lit - tle lamb whose fleece was white as snow.

Begin 4 on E	Begin 4 on A	Begin 4 on B	Three Black Keys	HT (Hands Together)

Teacher Accompaniment. Swing quavers. Student begins on the E an octave above Middle C.

F G A B WALTZ

UNIT 2
ROTE

Hague

Check off when mastered.

LH RH
5 4 3 2   1 2 3 4

Teacher Accompaniment

RIVER RAFTING

UNIT 2
READING

Allegro

Hague & Fisher

I stare down in - to the wa - ter. Waves are lap - ping past my raft.

Rush - ing wa - ter swirls in cir - cles. Twirl - ing, whirl - ing round and round.

Teacher Accompaniment. Student begins on the F above Middle C.

Allegro is the Italian word for happy. In music, it means to play fast.

rit. is the abbreviation for *ritardando*. In Italian it means to slow down gradually.

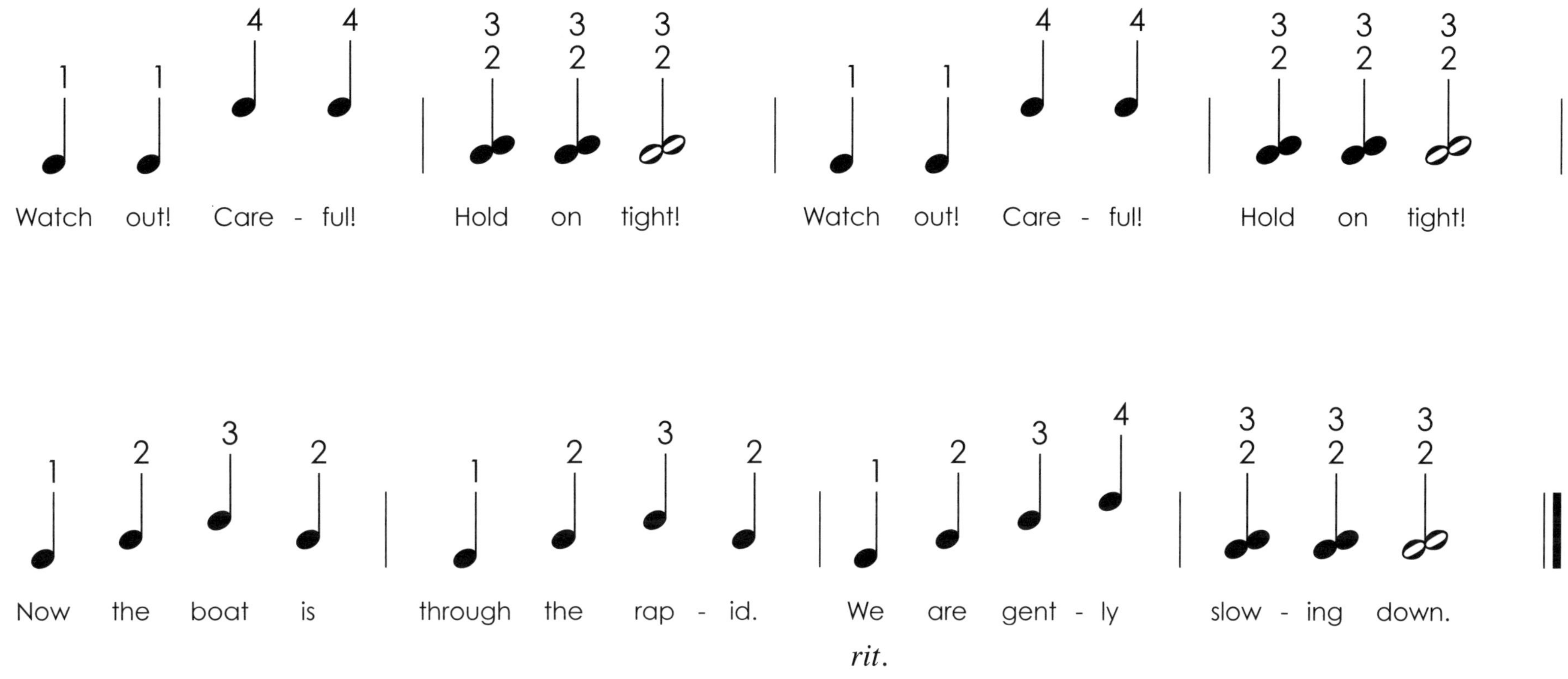

Watch out! Care - ful! Hold on tight! Watch out! Care - ful! Hold on tight!

Now the boat is through the rap - id. We are gent - ly slow - ing down.
rit.

rit.

TALL GIRAFFE
Left Hand

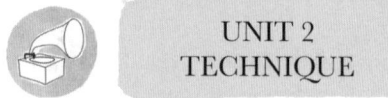

UNIT 2
TECHNIQUE

Hague & Fisher

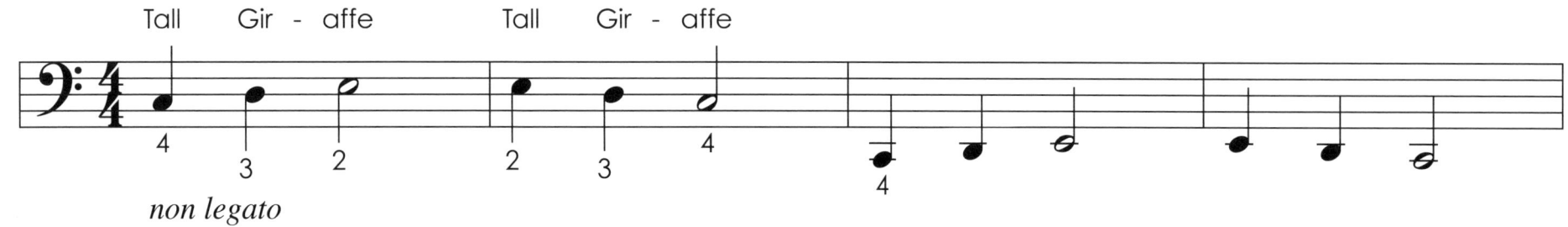

non legato

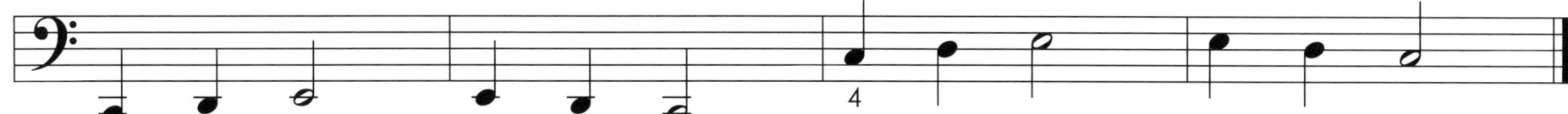

Tall Giraffe is at the top of the hill.

He walks down the hill and eats leaves from a tree.

And walks back up the hill.

DO YOU HAVE?

- *Non legato* articulation
- A graceful wrist lift on the minims

Teacher Accompaniment

non legato

TALL GIRAFFE
Right Hand

UNIT 2
TECHNIQUE

Hague & Fisher

non legato

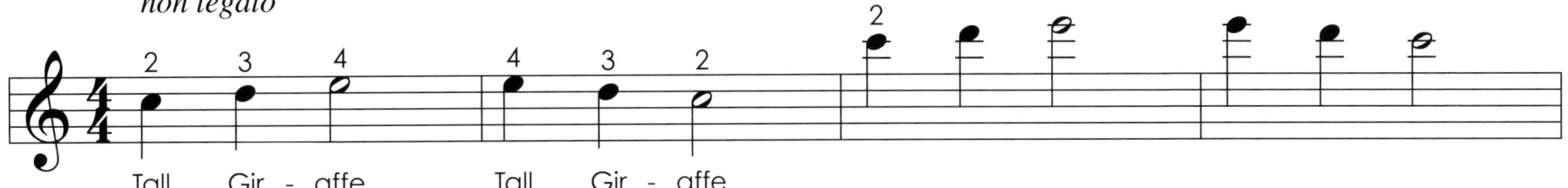

Tall   Gir - affe   Tall   Gir - affe

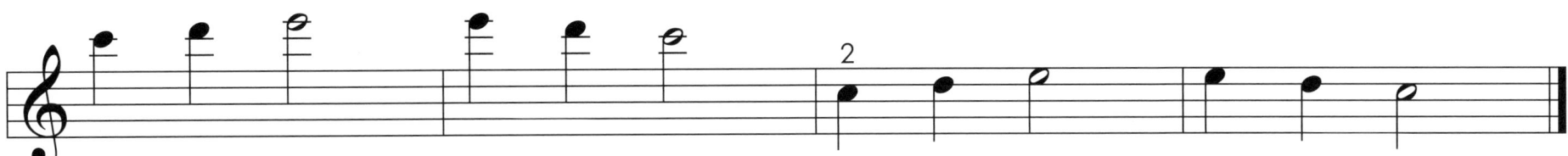

I am a small giraffe...

Sometimes I imagine what it would be like to be big!

It would be fun to eat leaves from the very top of the tree!

But right now, I am a small giraffe.

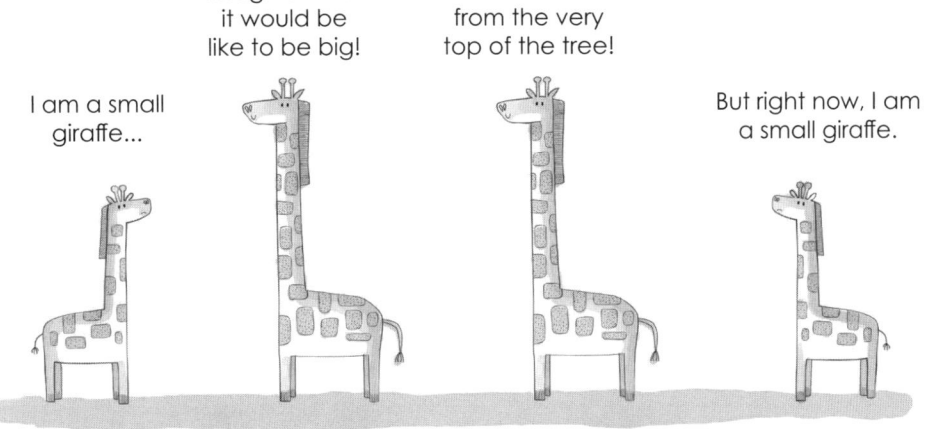

Non legato means "not connected" in Italian. Use a small arm bounce on each note to create disconnected sounds.

Teacher Accompaniment

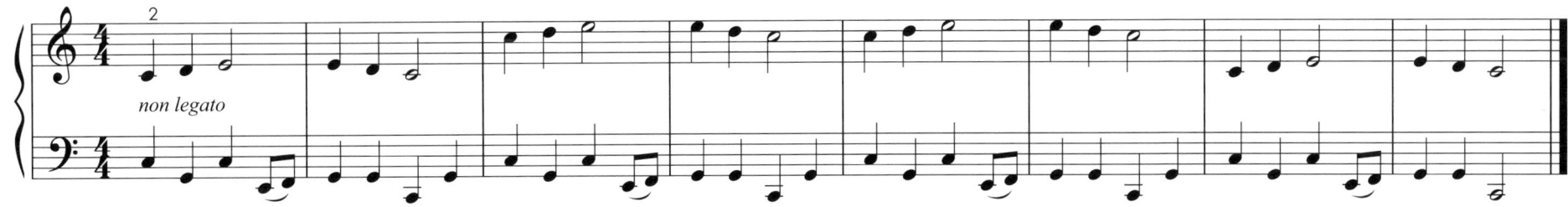

TALL GIRAFFE AND FRIENDS

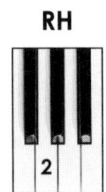

Teacher:

After playing as written, improvise different phrases for the student to echo.

UNIT 2
IMPROVISATION

Swing quavers

Joey Lieber

Student

Teacher

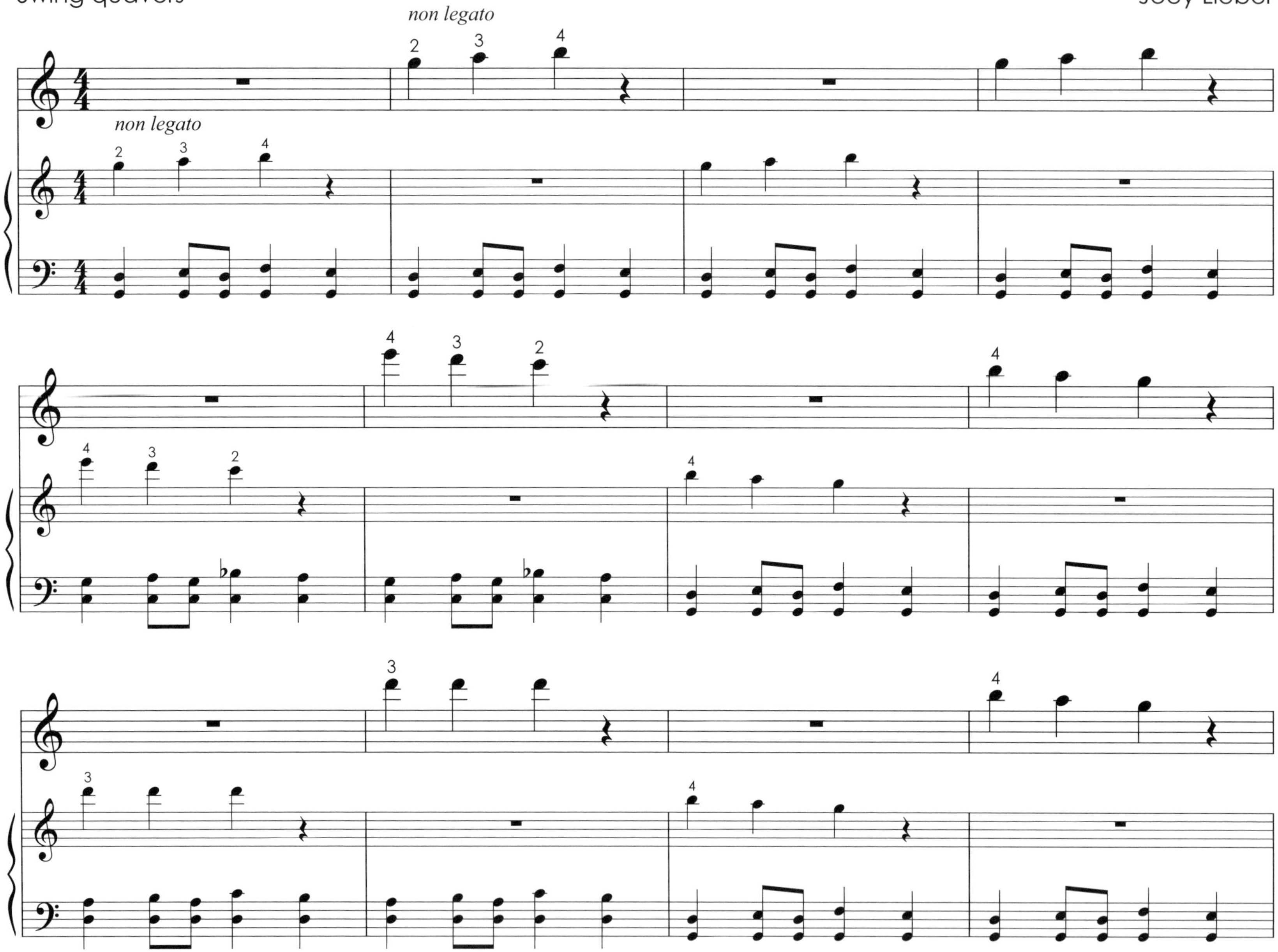

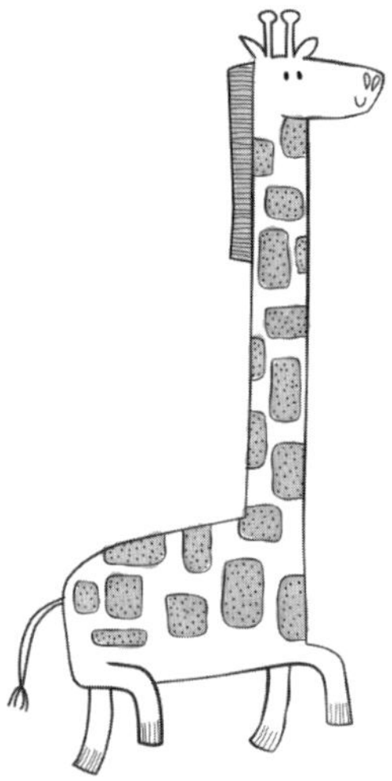

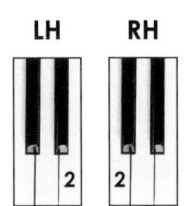

A DAY IN THE LIFE OF A TALL GIRAFFE

Moderato

Hague

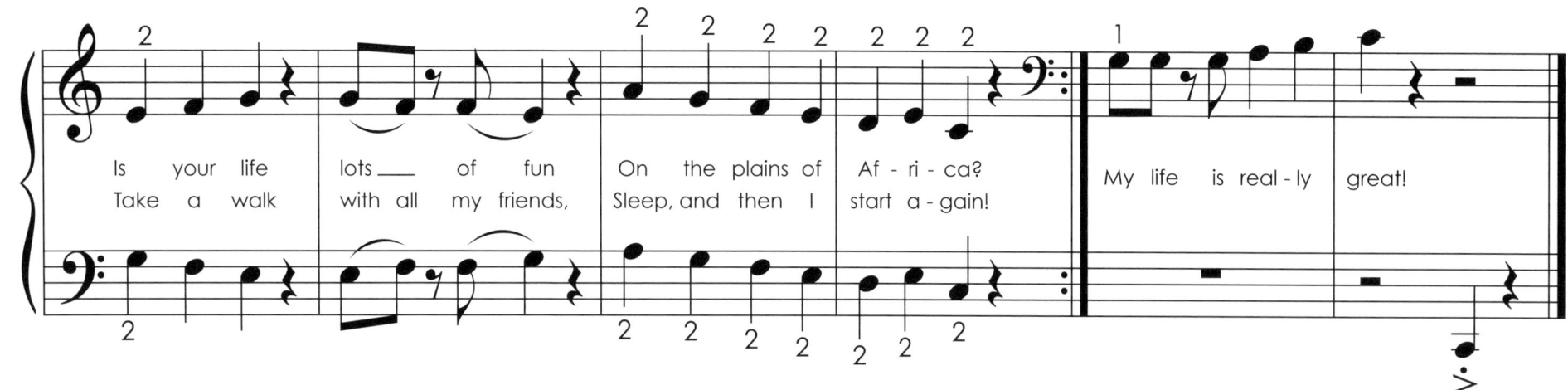

FUZZY WUZZY

UNIT 2 READING

Hague, Lyrics Traditional

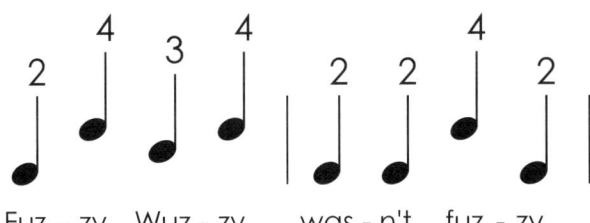
Fuz - zy Wuz - zy was - n't fuz - zy.

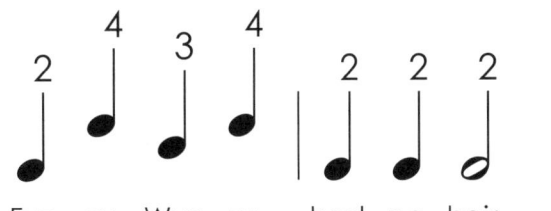
Fuz - zy Wuz - zy had no hair.

Andante

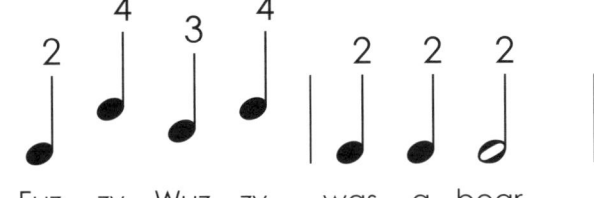
Fuz - zy Wuz - zy was a bear.

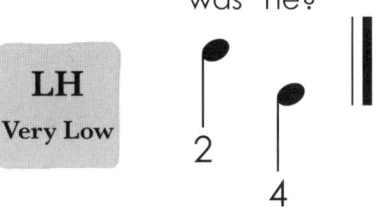
was he?

Begin 2 on C

3 Black Keys

Andante is the Italian word that means "to walk."

Teacher Accompaniment. Student begins on Middle C.

55

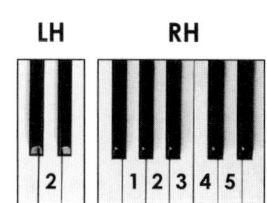

ODE TO JOY

Joyfully

Beethoven, arr. Hague

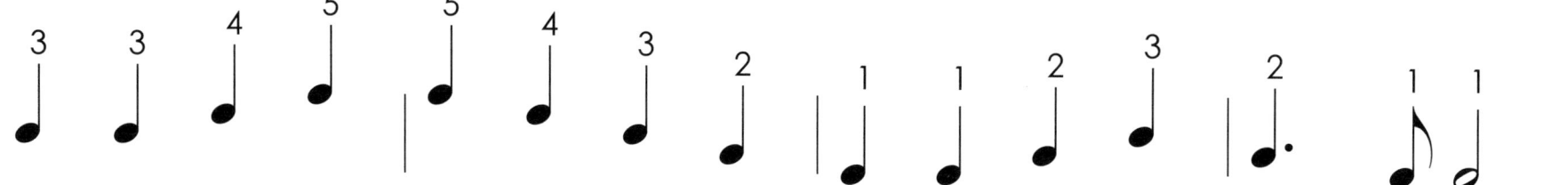

𝅘𝅥𝅭 𝅘𝅥𝅮 rhythm should be taught by rote.

Teacher Accompaniment. Student begins on the B above Middle C.

UNIT 2
READING

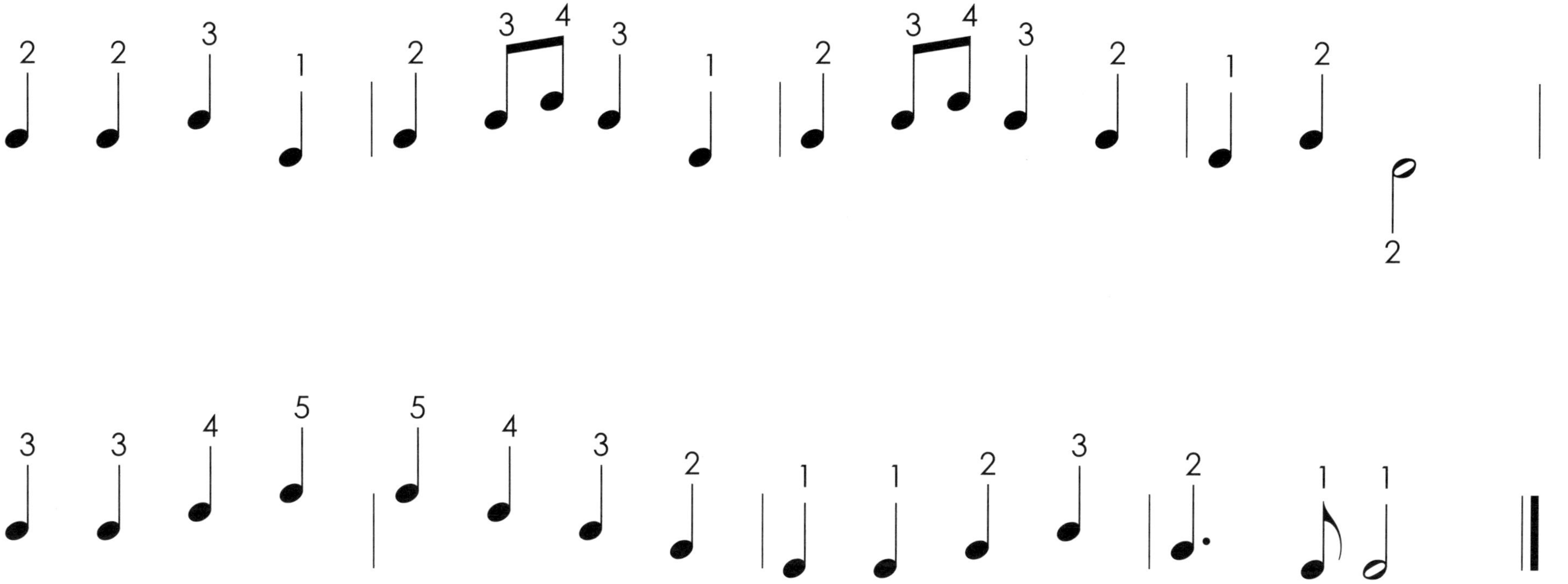

Begin RH 3 on B
LH on D

Begin RH 3 on E
LH on G

ROBOTS

UNIT 2
ROTE

Adagio

Hague

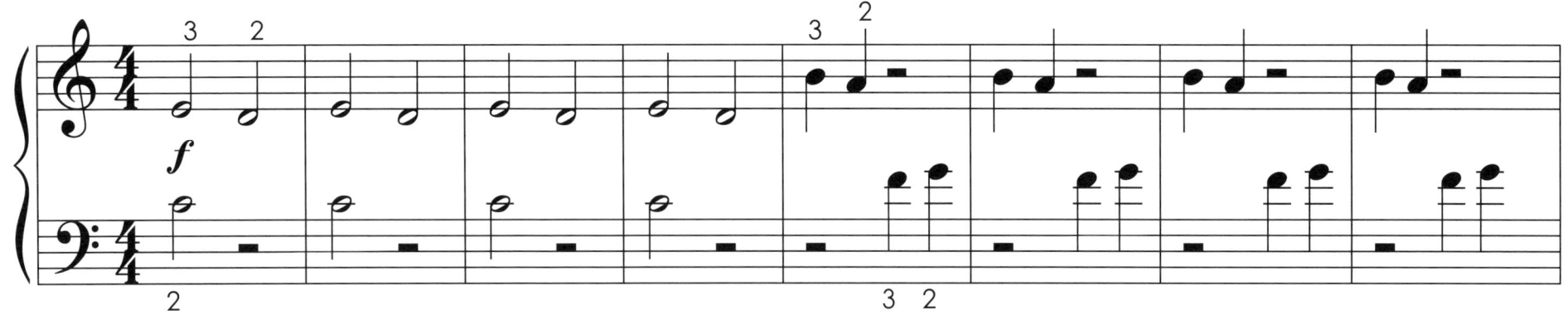

Andante

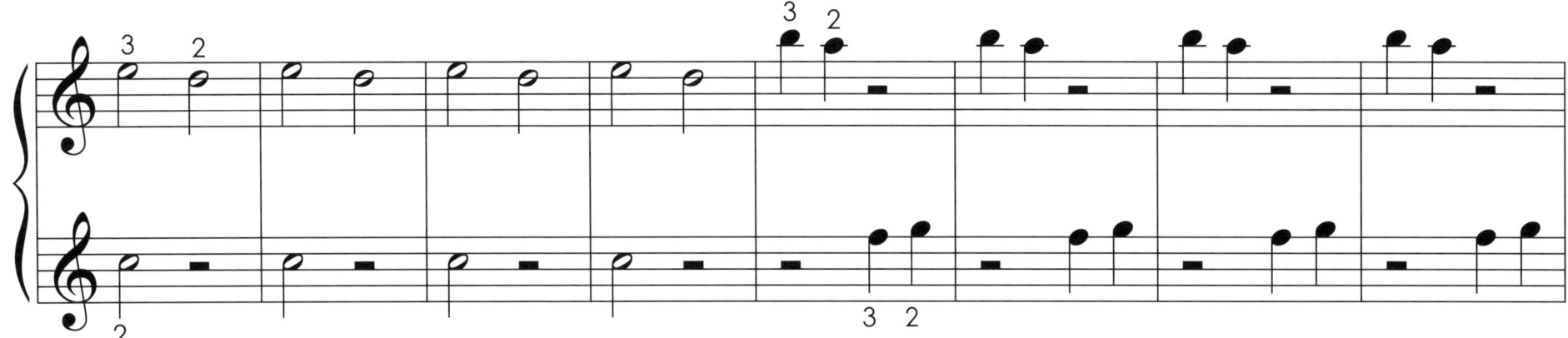

Adagio is the Italian word for slow.

Allegro

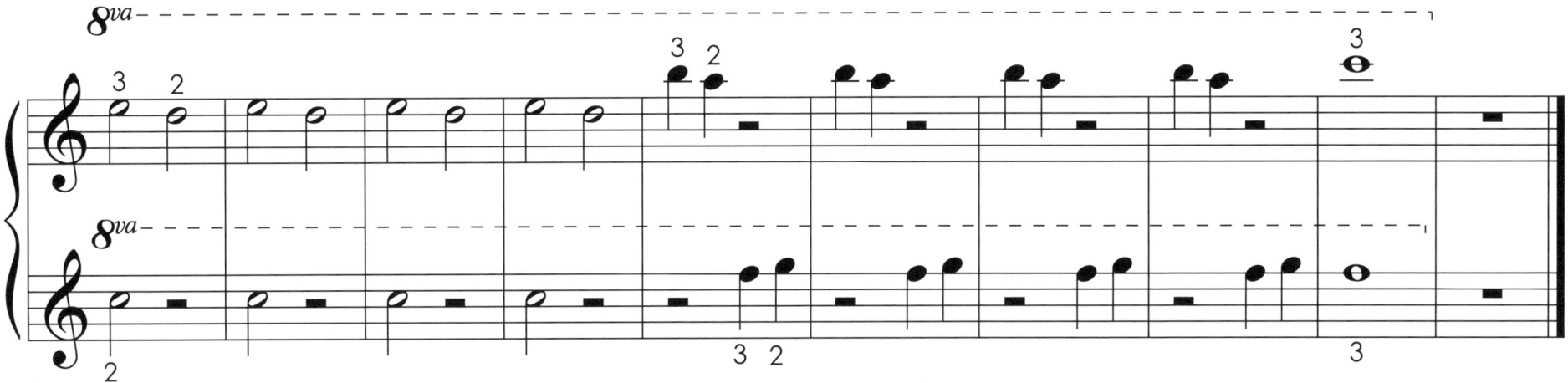

Teacher Accompaniment

STAVE

UNIT 3
THEORY

Music notation is written on a **Stave** of spaces and lines.

Space Note 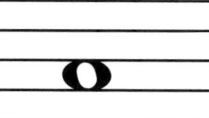   **Line Note**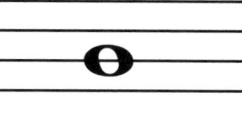

Colour the Space Notes blue and Line Notes red.

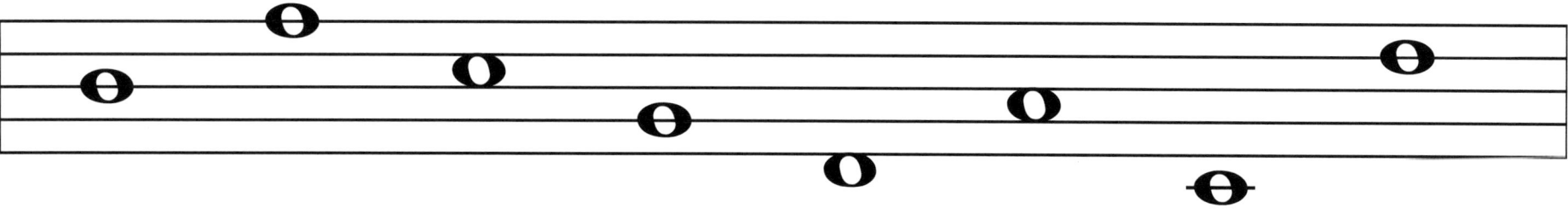

Write Space Notes.

Write Line Notes.

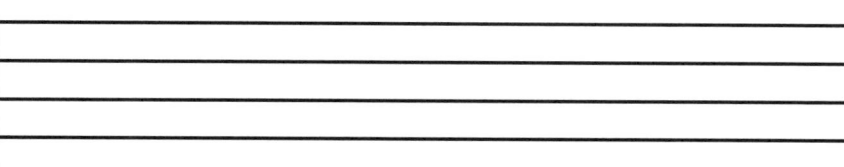

Assign **Piano Safari Sight Reading & Rhythm Cards Level C** during Unit 3.

Treble Clef shows notes in the upper range of the piano. It is usually played by the **RH**.

Bass Clef shows notes in the lower range of the piano. It is usually played by the **LH**.

Time Signature shows how many beats are in each bar of the piece.

How many lines are in the **Treble Stave**? _____   How many lines are in the **Bass Stave**? _____

Write a row of **Treble Clef** signs on the top stave and **Bass Clef** signs on the bottom stave.

61

LANDMARKS

UNIT 3
THEORY

Treble G is in the Treble Clef on the **2nd line up**. It is usually played by the **RH**. Colour the Treble Clef sign red.
Write three Treble G's.

Bass C is in the Bass Clef on the **2nd space up**. It is usually played by the **LH**. Colour the Bass Clef sign blue.
Write three Bass C's.

Middle C is the C in the middle of the keyboard.

Treble G is the G above Middle C. Colour it red on the keyboard below.

Bass C is the C below Middle C. Colour it blue on the keyboard below.

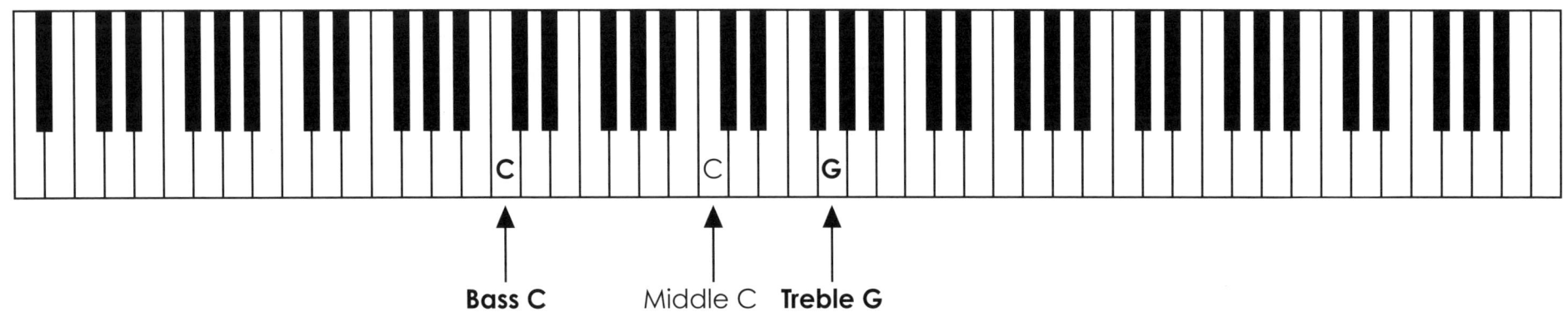

THE INTERVAL OF A 2ND

UNIT 3
THEORY

An **Interval** is the distance between two notes.

When two notes are the interval of a **2nd** apart, they move
from a line to the next space or from a space to the next line.

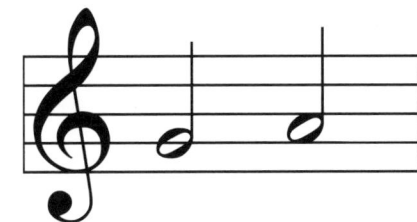

Melodic 2nds are played consecutively.

Harmonic 2nds are played together.

Play G. Play ↗ 2nd ↗ 2nd ↘ 2nd ↘ 2nd ↗ 2nd. What note did you end on? _____

Write 2nds up or down from the following notes.

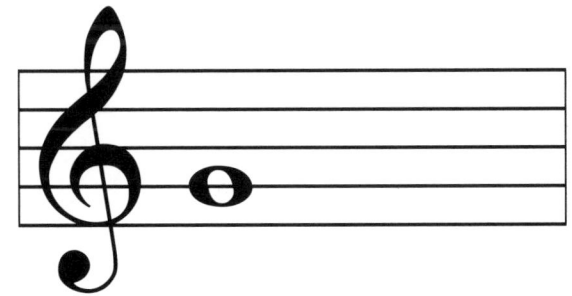

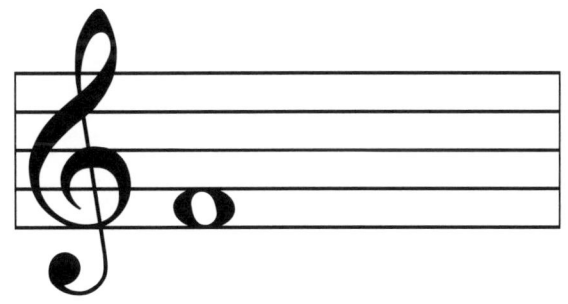

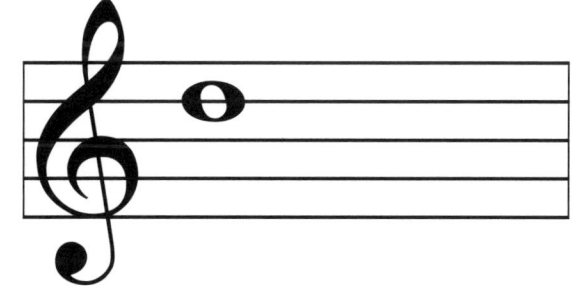

MY DOG FRITZ

UNIT 3
READING

Allegro

Hague

mf My dog Fritz is so much fun. I say, "Fetch!" and off he runs.

Fritz and I can play all day if the rain will stay a - way.

| *mf* | **mezzo forte** means to play medium loud. | | *8va* | Play one octave higher than written. |

Teacher Accompaniment

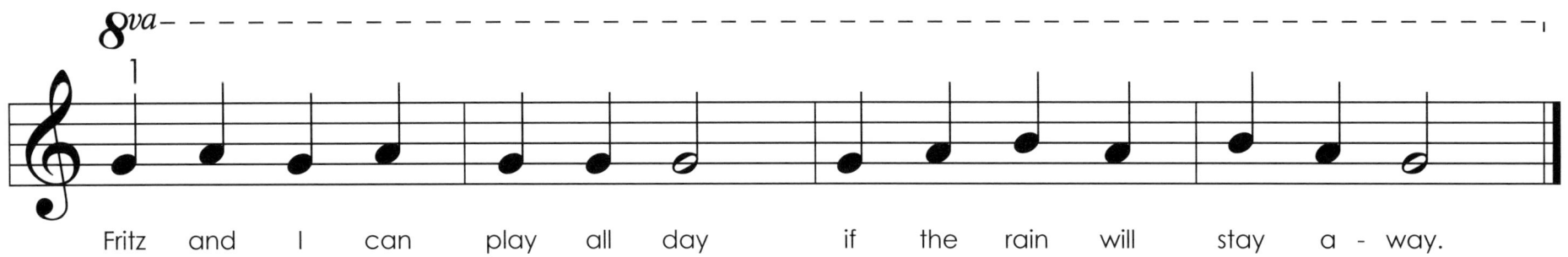

CREEPY BASEMENT

UNIT 3
READING

Andante

Hague & Stevens

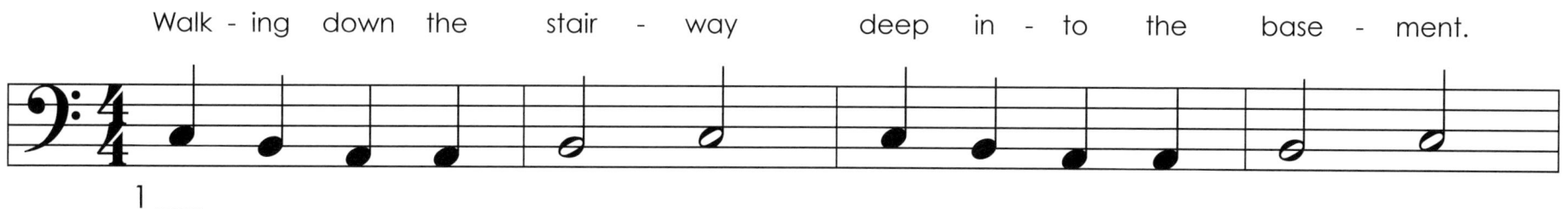

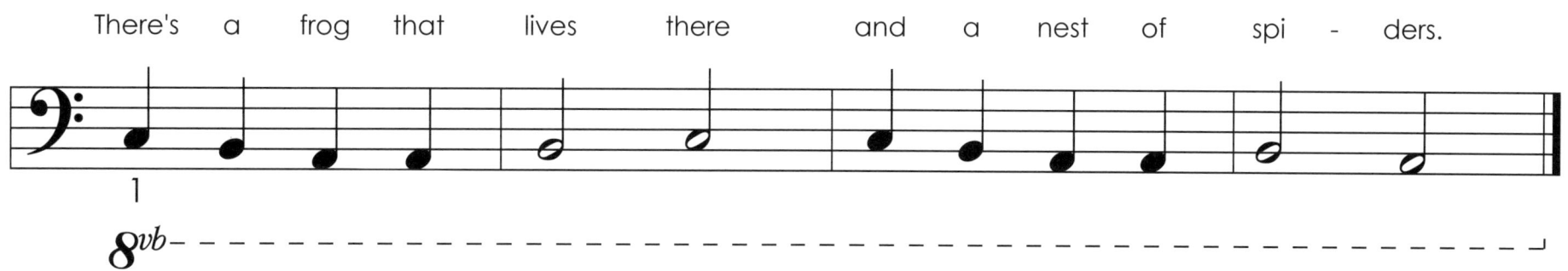

8vb Play one octave lower than written.

Teacher Accompaniment

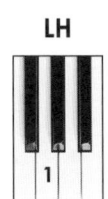

ZECHARIAH ZEBRA
Left Hand

UNIT 3
TECHNIQUE

Hague

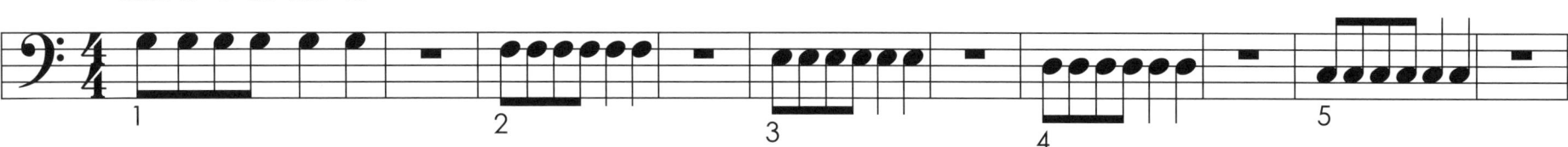

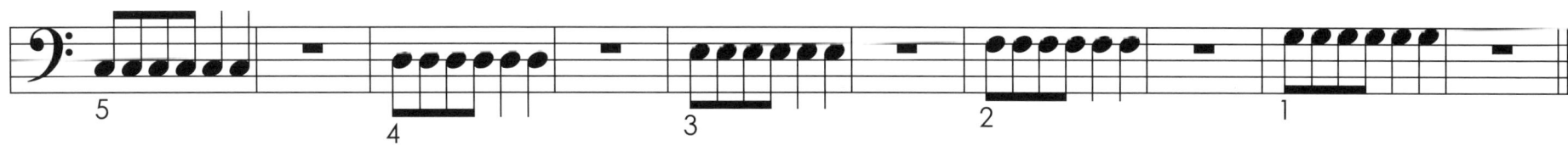

Teacher Accompaniment

ZECHARIAH ZEBRA
Right Hand

DO YOU HAVE?
- Small bounces on the "Zechariah" notes and higher bounces on the "Zebra" notes
- Thumb on the corner tip
- Firm fingertips
- A correct piano hand shape

UNIT 3
TECHNIQUE

Hague

Zech-a - ri - ah Zeb - ra

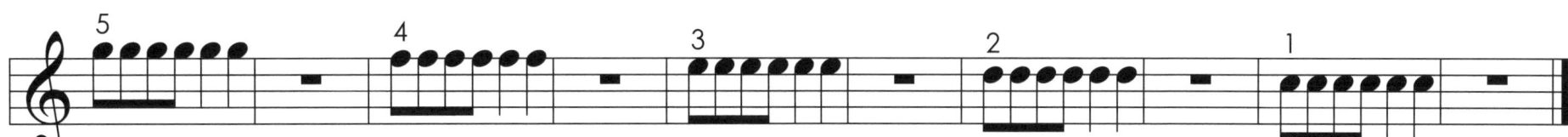

Teacher Accompaniment

simile

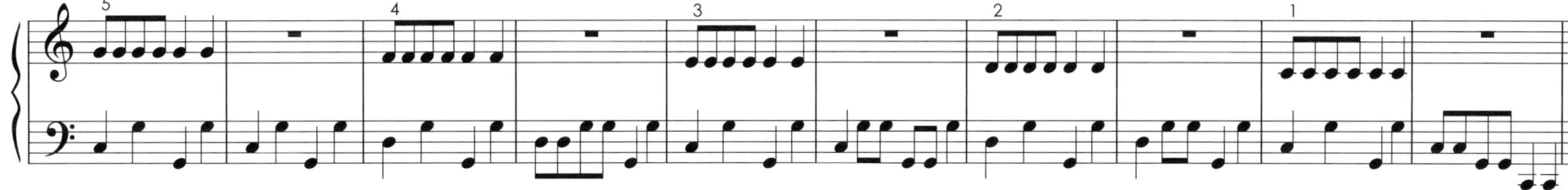

ZEBRA ON THE PLAYGROUND

UNIT 3
IMPROVISATION

Step 1 Learn the Zechariah Zebra Pattern below, and play it on different white keys using RH Finger 2.

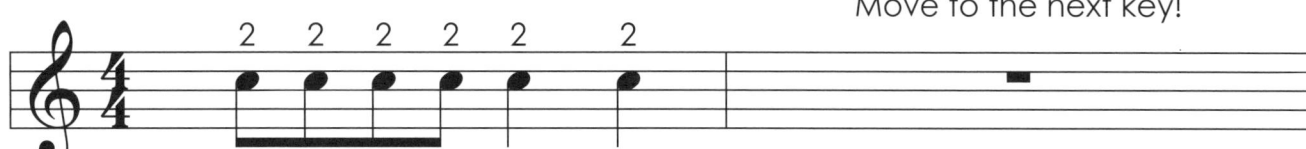

Step 2

Write C, E, or G in each box:

Zechariah runs over to the slide!

Write F, A, or C:

Zechariah jumps on the trampoline.

Write C, E, or G:

It is time for the swings!
Zechariah swings so high he feels like he is flying.

Step 3 — With RH Finger 2, play the Zechariah Zebra Pattern in order of the notes you chose in Step 2 while your teacher plays the accompaniment.

Step 4 — Colour RH Finger 2 in the picture below. Choose another finger, repeat Step 3 with that finger, and colour it in the picture below. Repeat with all the fingers until the hands are completely coloured!

Teacher Accompaniment

Hague

ZEBRA ON A POGO STICK

UNIT 3
ROTE

Moderato

Hague

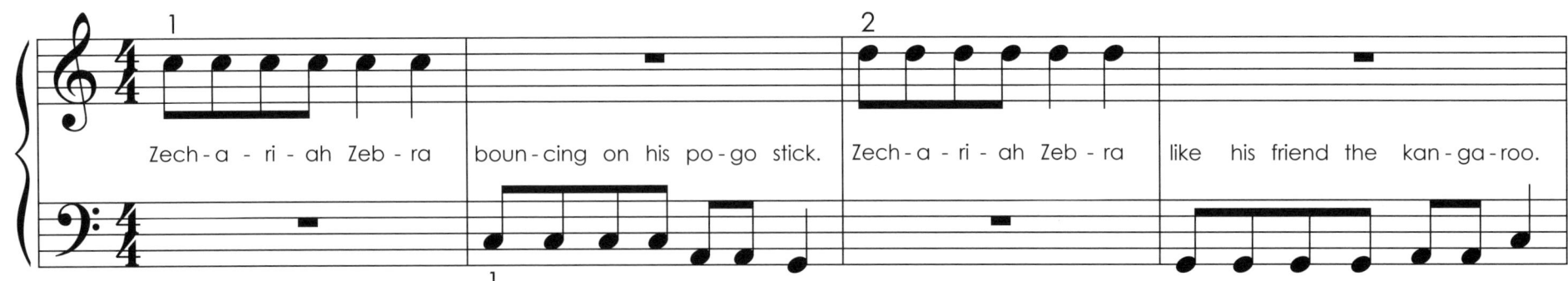

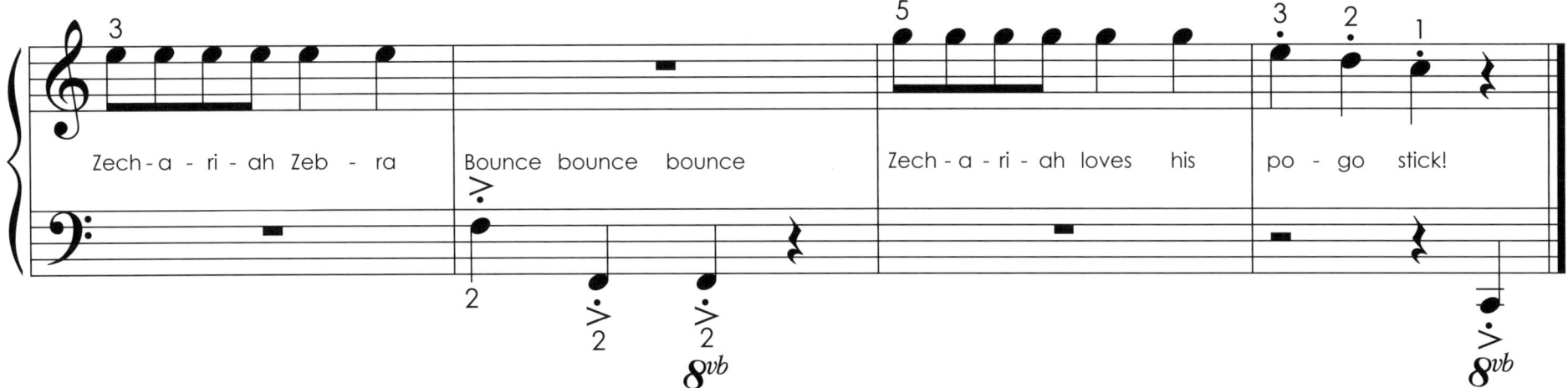

Teacher Accompaniment. Student plays one octave higher than written.

CITY STROLL

Allegro

Fisher & Fisher

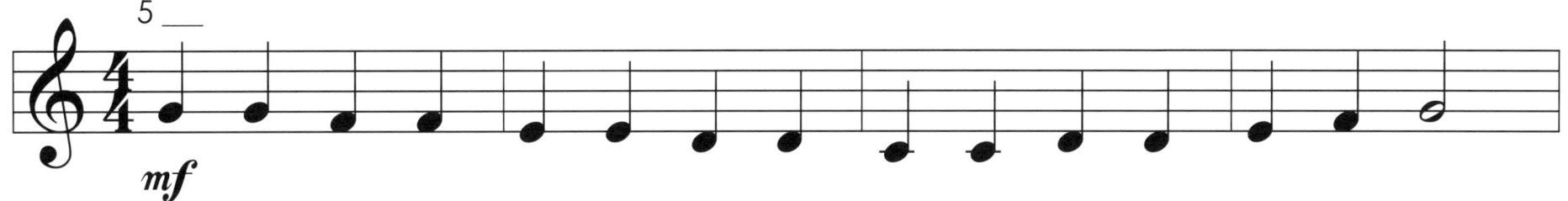

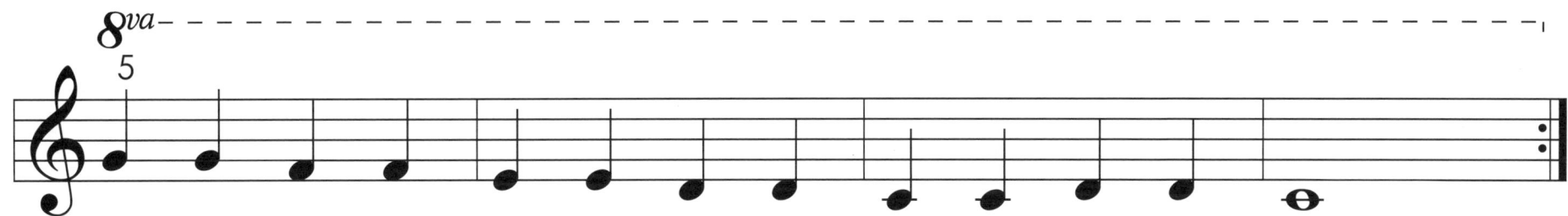

Teacher Accompaniment. Swing quavers. Student plays one octave higher than written.

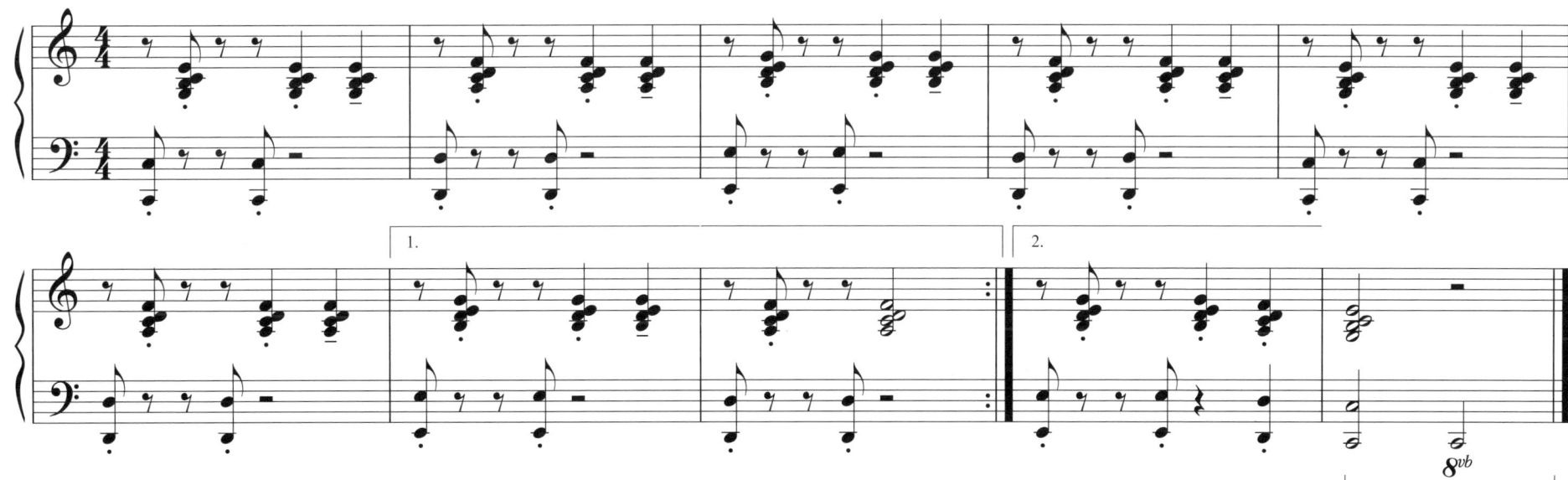

UNIT 3
READING

CHICKEN CHATTER

UNIT 3
READING

Allegro

Fisher & Fisher

Repeat 8va

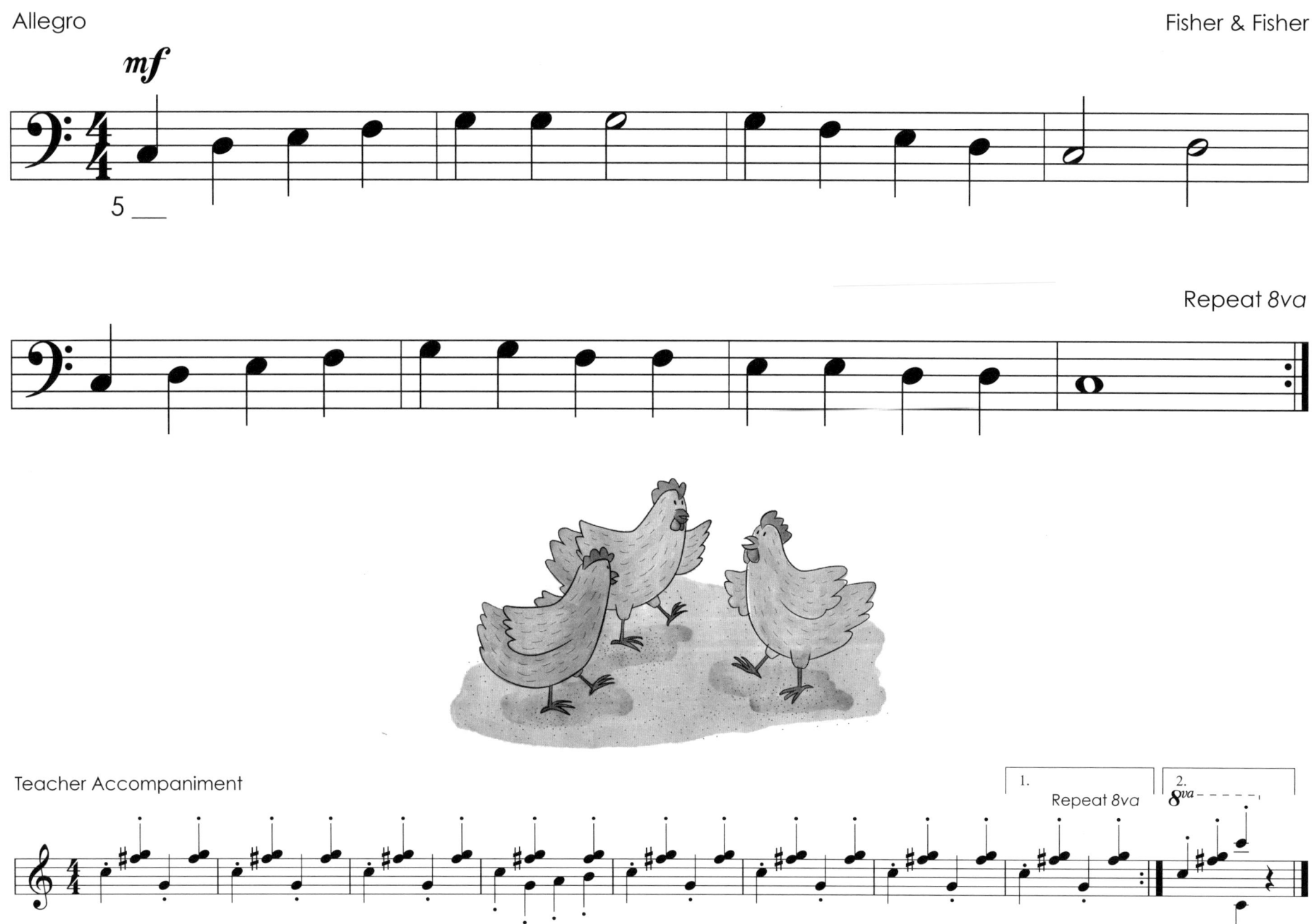

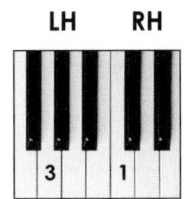

BINGO

Moderato

**UNIT 3
FOLK**

English Folk Song, arr. Hague

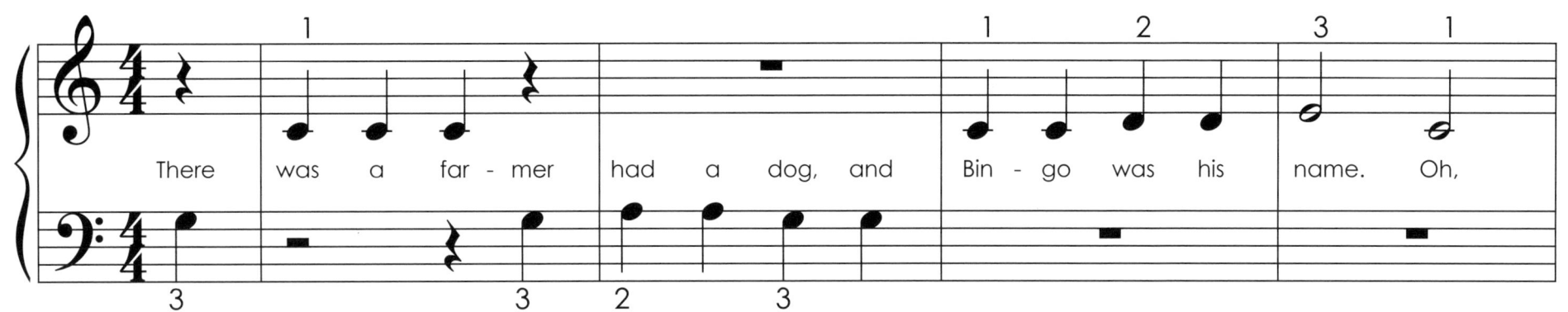

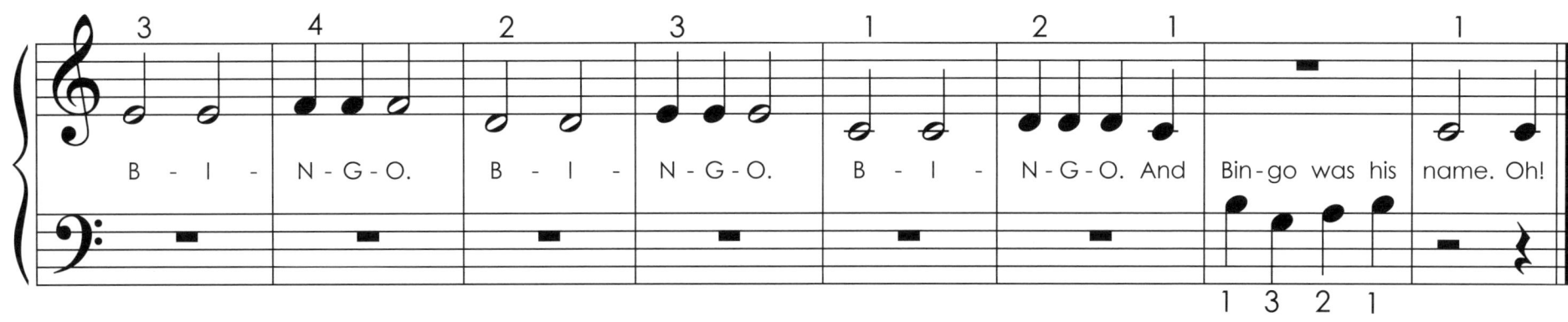

Teacher Accompaniment. Student plays one octave higher than written.

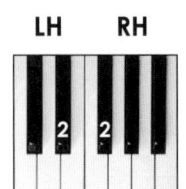

DANDELION FLUFF

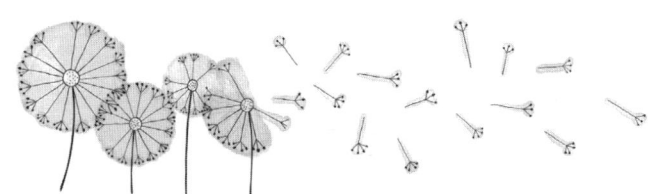

UNIT 3 ROTE

Andante

Hague & C. Fisher

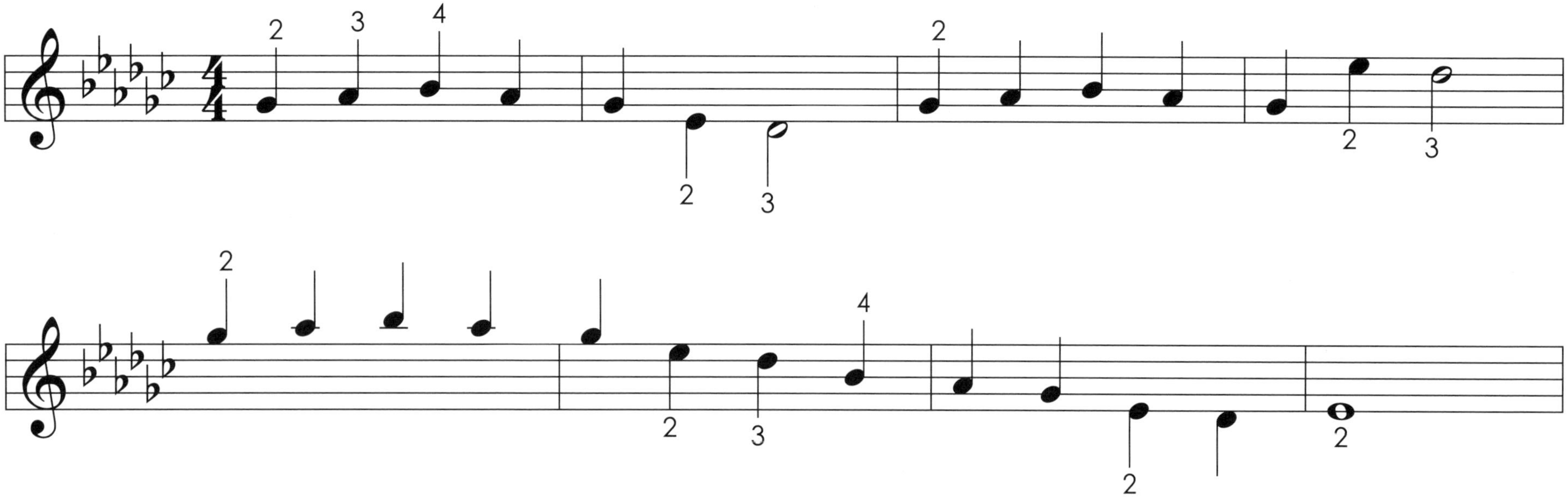

Teacher Accompaniment. Student plays one octave higher than written.

con pedale

KRISTABEL KANGAROO

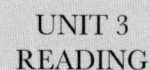
UNIT 3
READING

Moderato   Fisher & Hague

Kris - ta - bel   Kan - ga - roo   wants   to   fly.

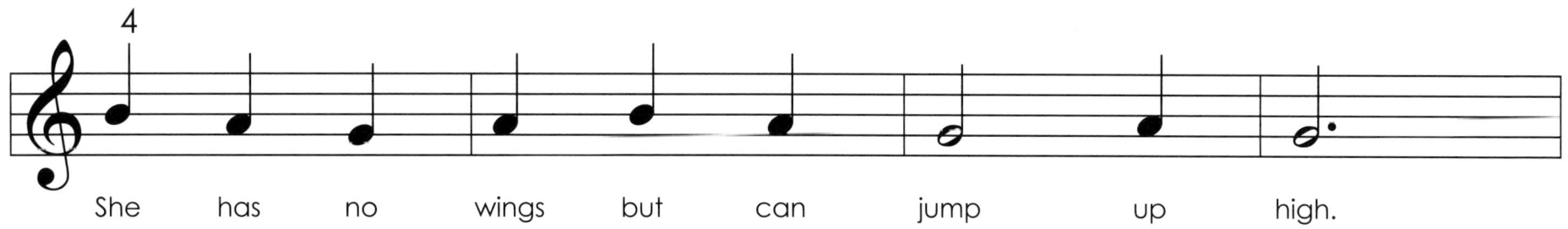

She   has   no   wings   but   can   jump   up   high.

A **Dotted Minim** equals three beats. When you see it, say "Ta - 2 - 3."

Teacher Accompaniment

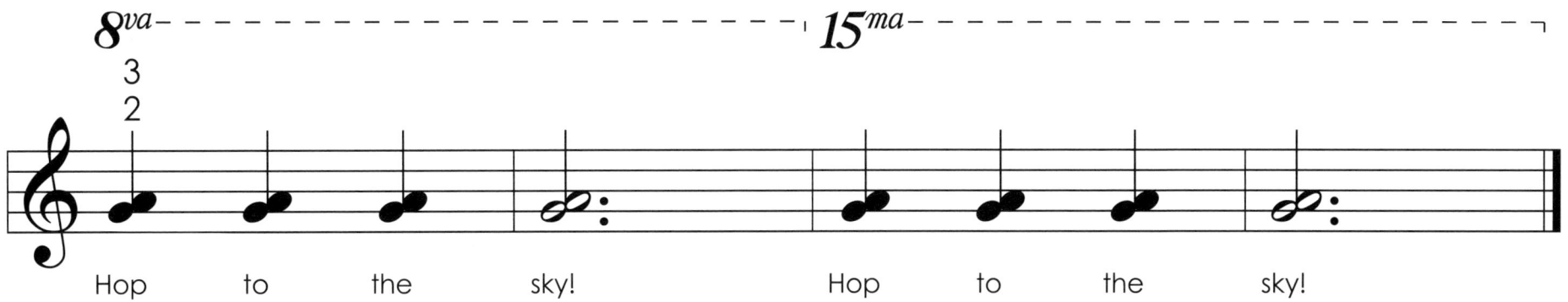

15ma Play two octaves higher than written.

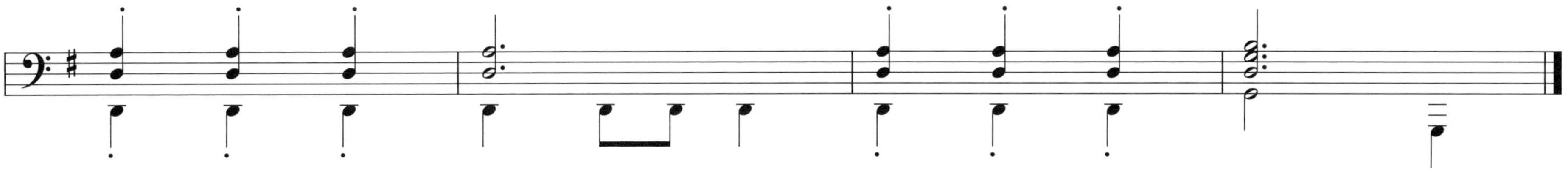

WEIRD BIRD

UNIT 3
READING

A **Semibreve Rest** equals an entire bar of silence. In 4/4, when you count it, whisper "Rest - 2 - 3 - 4."

MIDNIGHT WALTZ

Moderato

Fisher & Hague

UNIT 3
READING

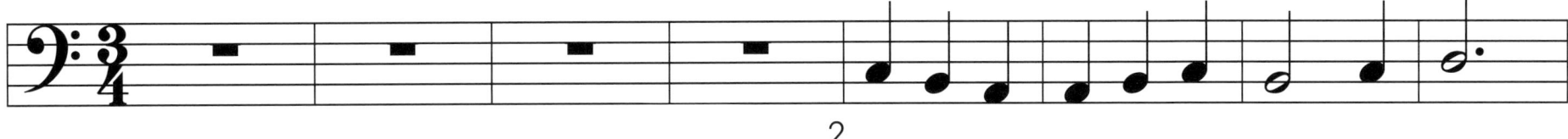

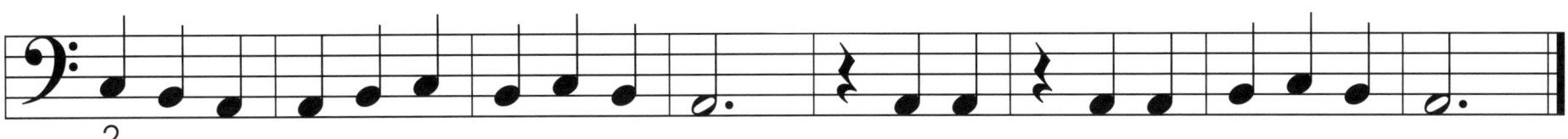

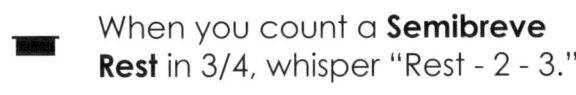 When you count a **Semibreve Rest** in 3/4, whisper "Rest - 2 - 3."

𝄽 A **Crotchet Rest** equals one beat of silence. When you see it, whisper "Rest."

Teacher Accompaniment

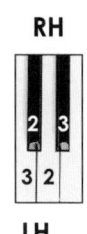

CROCODILE IN THE NILE

UNIT 3
ROTE

Allegro

Wendy Lynn Stevens

Croc - o - dile   in the Nile   does - n't   e - ver,   e - ver smile.

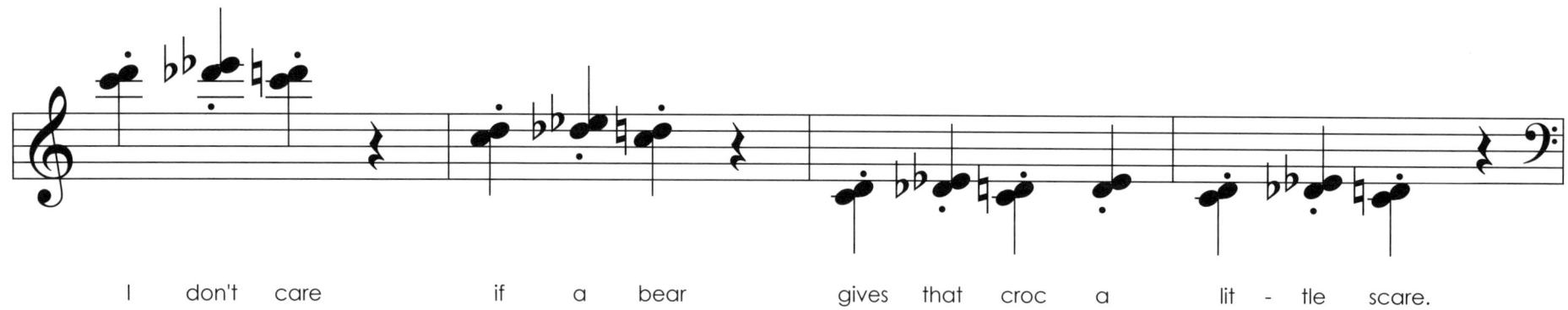

I don't care   if a bear   gives that croc a   lit - tle scare.

Copyright © 2009 by Wendy Lynn Stevens

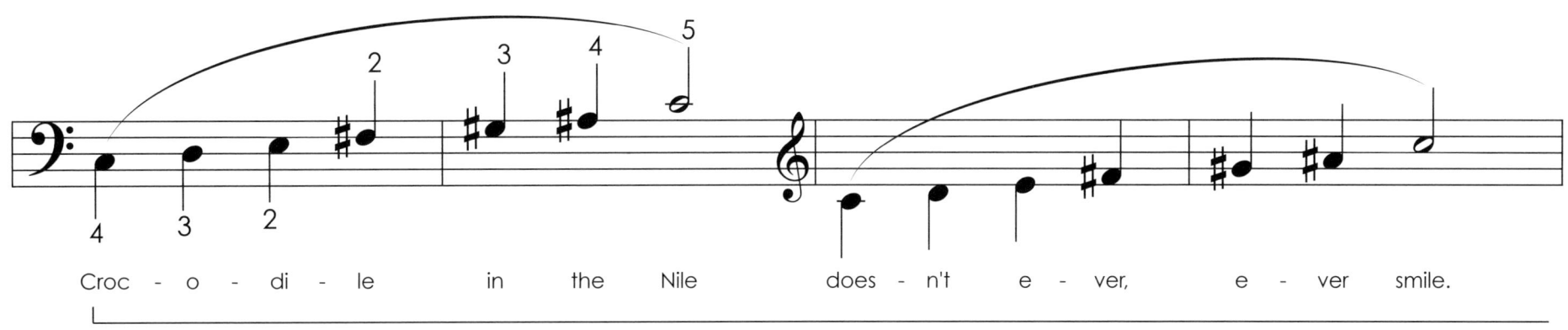
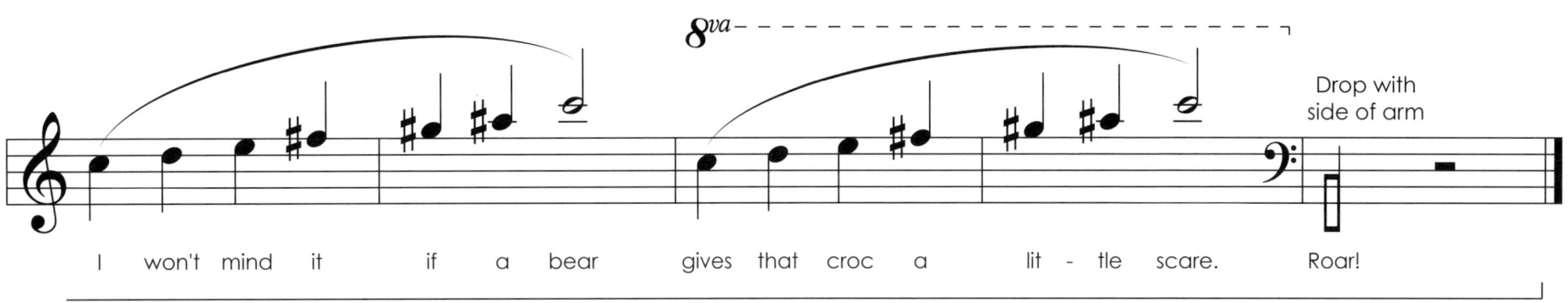
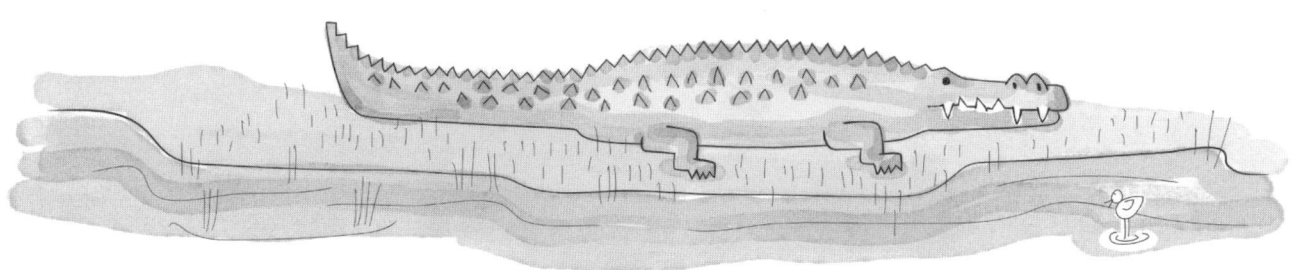

THUNDERSTORM OVER THE PRAIRIE

UNIT 3
IMPROVISATION

Step 1. Draw pictures in the boxes to match each part of the storm.
Step 2. Experiment on the piano to find sounds for each of the storm elements.
Step 3. Play the piece in the order of the boxes.

Gentle Rain	Hail	Thunder and Lightning	Heavy Rain

Thunder and Lightning	Distant Thunder	Sun Comes Out	Rainbow

Teacher Accompaniment. Repeat as necessary, and change between note values to match the student's improvisation. For example, at the beginning of the thunderstorm, play semibreves. As the thunderstorm becomes more violent, make the note values shorter.

Hague

THE INTERVAL OF A 3RD

UNIT 4 THEORY

When two notes are the interval of a **3rd** apart, they move from a line to the next line, or a space to the next space.

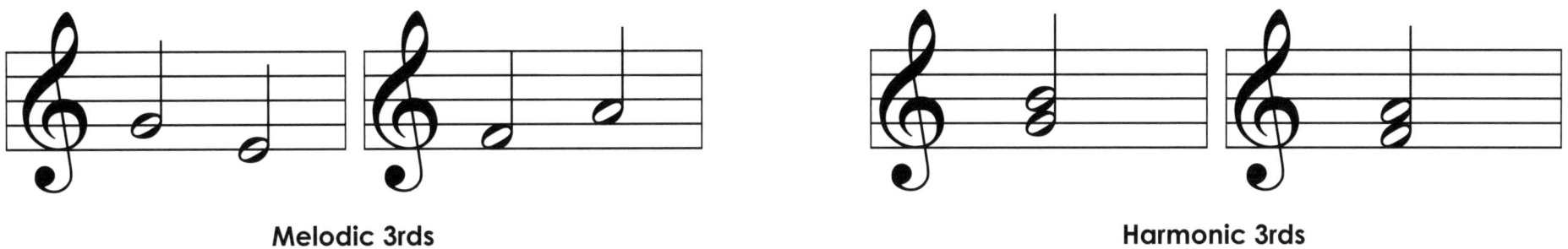

Melodic 3rds **Harmonic 3rds**

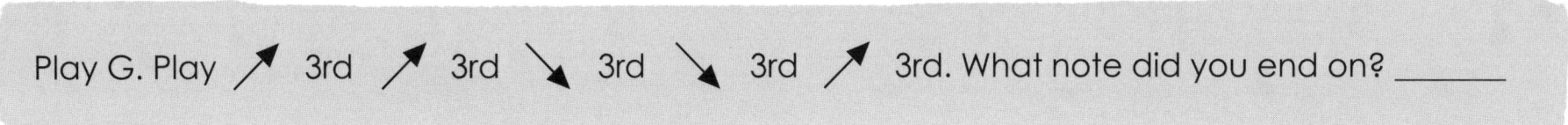

Write 3rds up or down from the following notes.

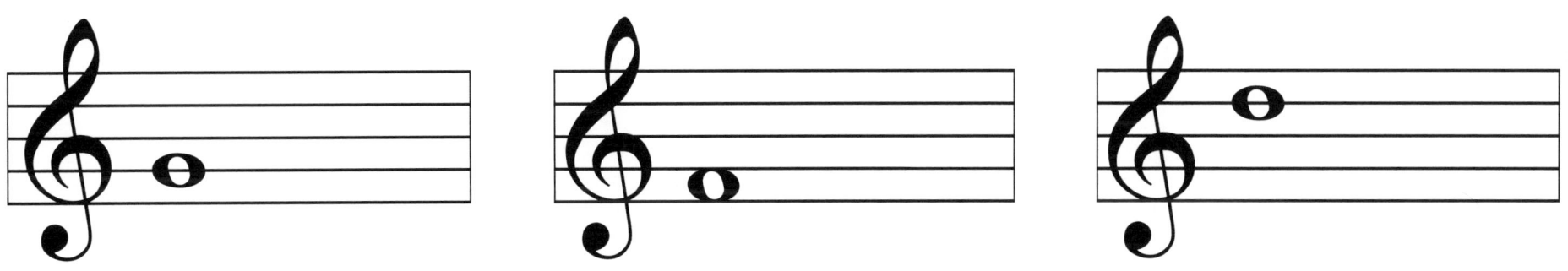

Assign Piano Safari Sight Reading & Rhythm Cards Level D during Unit 4.

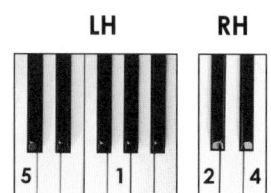

SKIP TO MY LOU
Secondo

 UNIT 4 ROTE

American Folk Song, arr. Hague

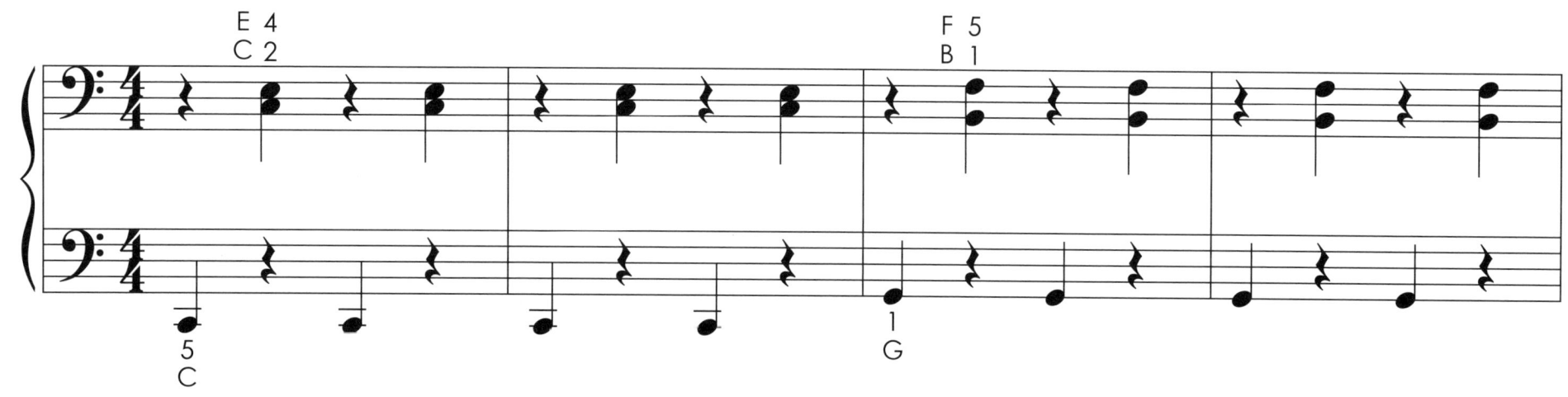

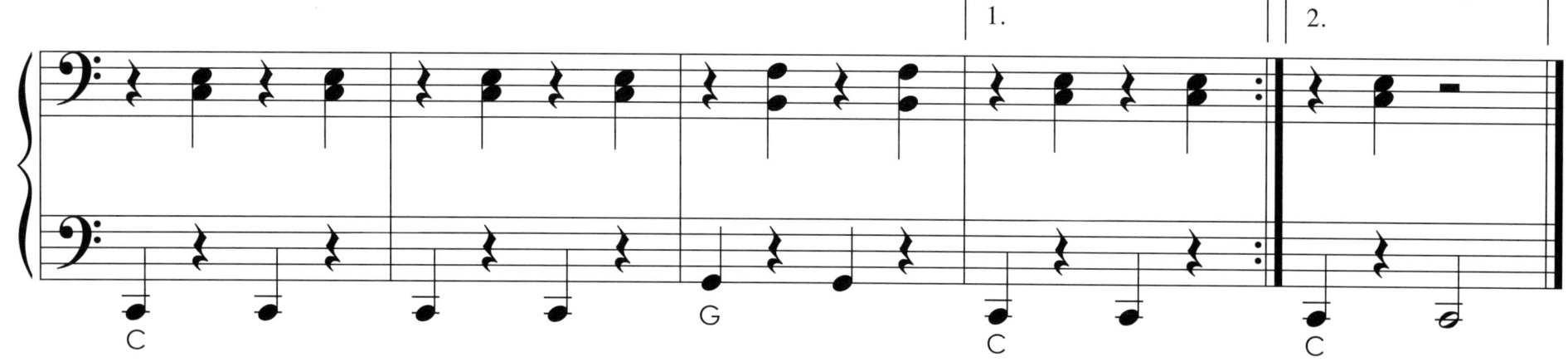

SKIP TO MY LOU
Primo

UNIT 4
ROTE

American Folk Song, arr. Hague

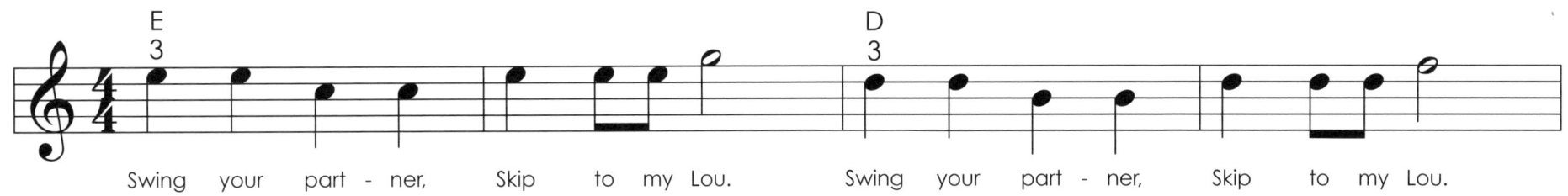

Swing your part-ner, Skip to my Lou. Swing your part-ner, Skip to my Lou.

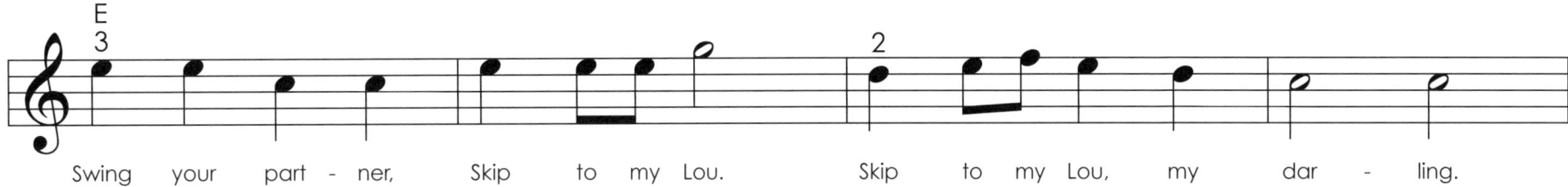

Swing your part-ner, Skip to my Lou. Skip to my Lou, my dar - ling.

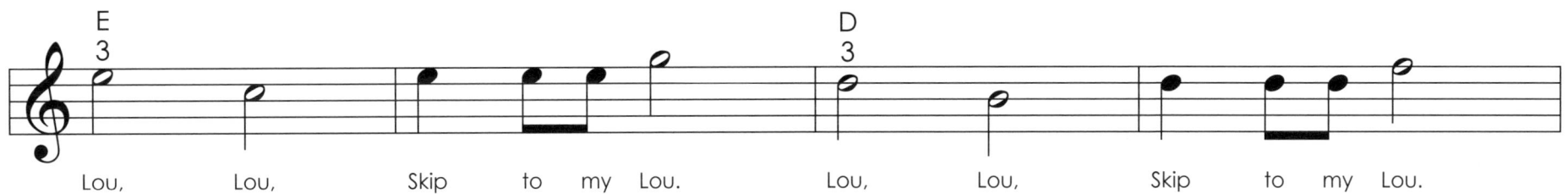

Lou, Lou, Skip to my Lou. Lou, Lou, Skip to my Lou.

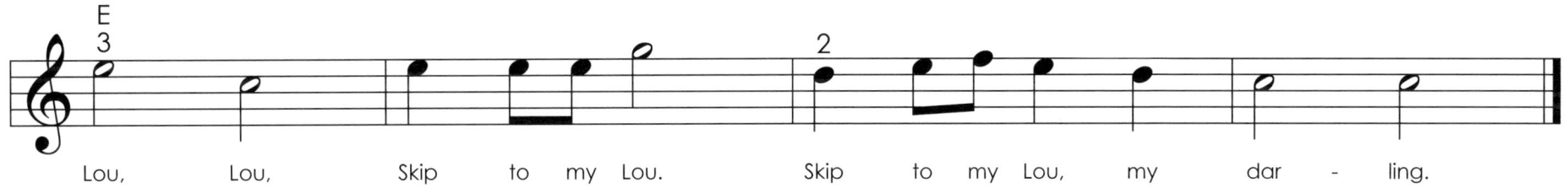

Lou, Lou, Skip to my Lou. Skip to my Lou, my dar - ling.

FERRIS WHEEL

Moderato

Hague & Fisher

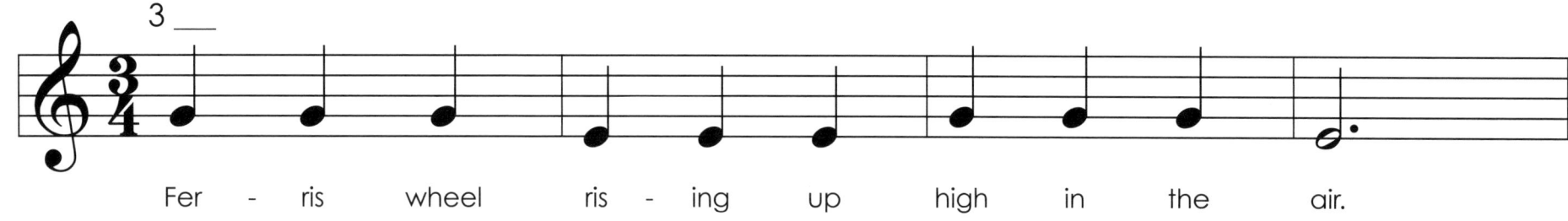

Fer - ris wheel ris - ing up high in the air.

This is what I love at the coun - ty fair.

Teacher Accompaniment

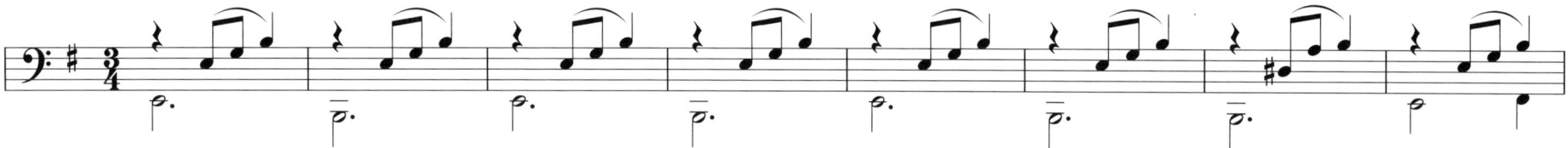

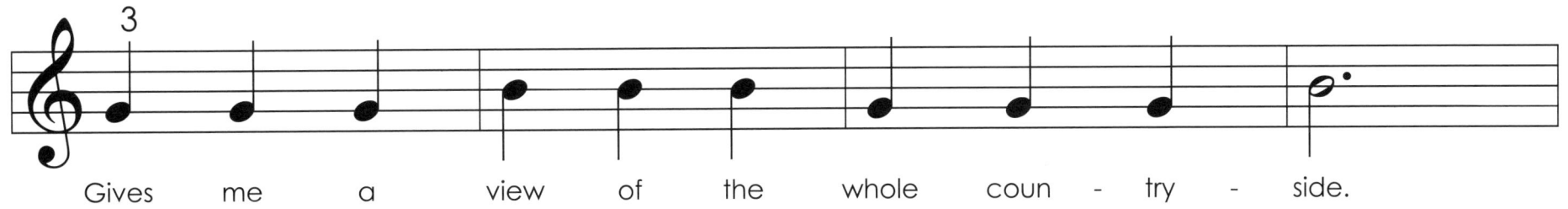
Gives me a view of the whole coun - try - side.

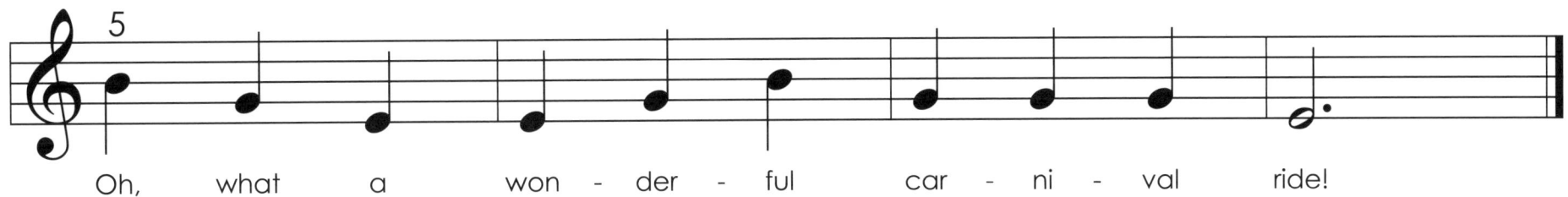
Oh, what a won - der - ful car - ni - val ride!

CHALLENGE!

Play Hands Together in parallel motion.
Begin with LH Finger 3 on G one octave
below the RH.

TREE FROG
Left Hand

UNIT 4
TECHNIQUE

Hague

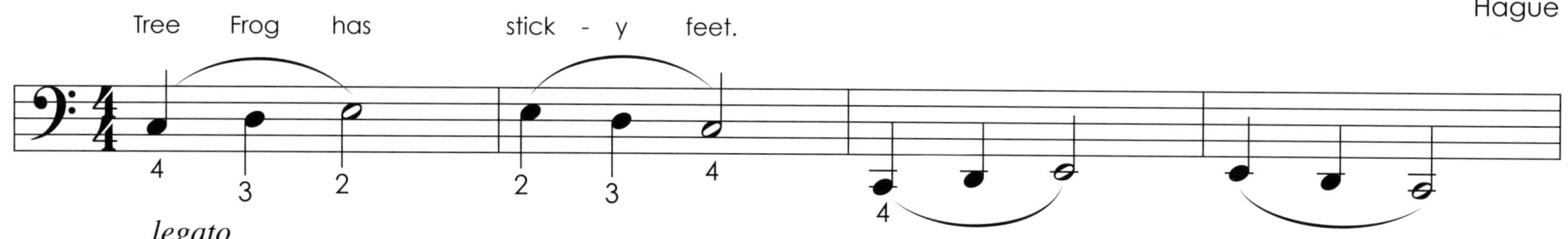

Tree Frog has stick-y feet.

legato

The notes in the Tree Frog Technique are the same as in Tall Giraffe Technique. However, Tree Frog is played *legato*, while Tall Giraffe is played *non legato*.

Create a story that shows how the Tree Frog moves up and down the octaves of this exercise.

Teacher Accompaniment

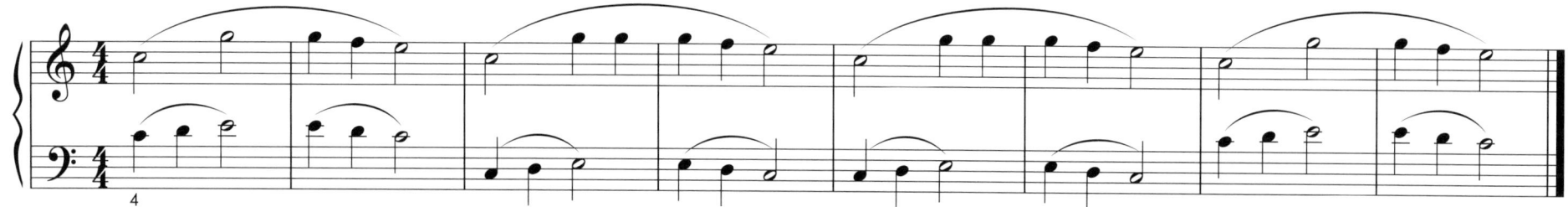

TREE FROG
Right Hand

UNIT 4
TECHNIQUE

Hague

legato

Tree Frog has stick - y feet.

DO YOU HAVE?

- Connected fingers in the *legato* articulation, with a small arm bounce on each note
- Graceful wrist lift at the end of each phrase
- Firm fingertips

Legato is the Italian word that means to play in a smooth and connected manner.

Teacher Accompaniment

TREE FROG IN A RAINSTORM

Step 1

Learn this Tree Frog Pattern with the RH.

Hague & Fisher

Tree Frog sits under a leaf on the forest floor.
It is a grey and rainy day.

Step 2

While your teacher plays the accompaniment, play the Tree Frog Pattern above.

Next, continue improvising using the notes G A B C D. Play them in any order, and listen carefully for a clear and beautiful *legato* sound.

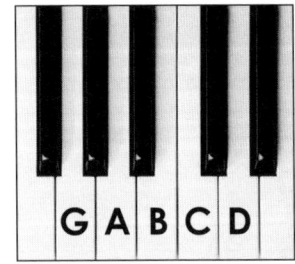

Tree Frog hops out from under the leaf to explore.

Step 3

End with this melody.

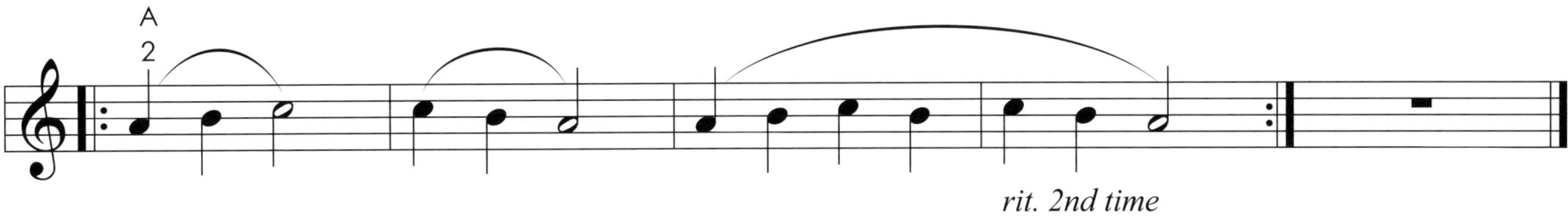

rit. 2nd time

Tree Frog retreats under his leaf to watch the rain.

TRY THIS!

- Change octaves.
- Vary the rhythm.
- Play hands together in parallel motion.

Teacher Accompaniment

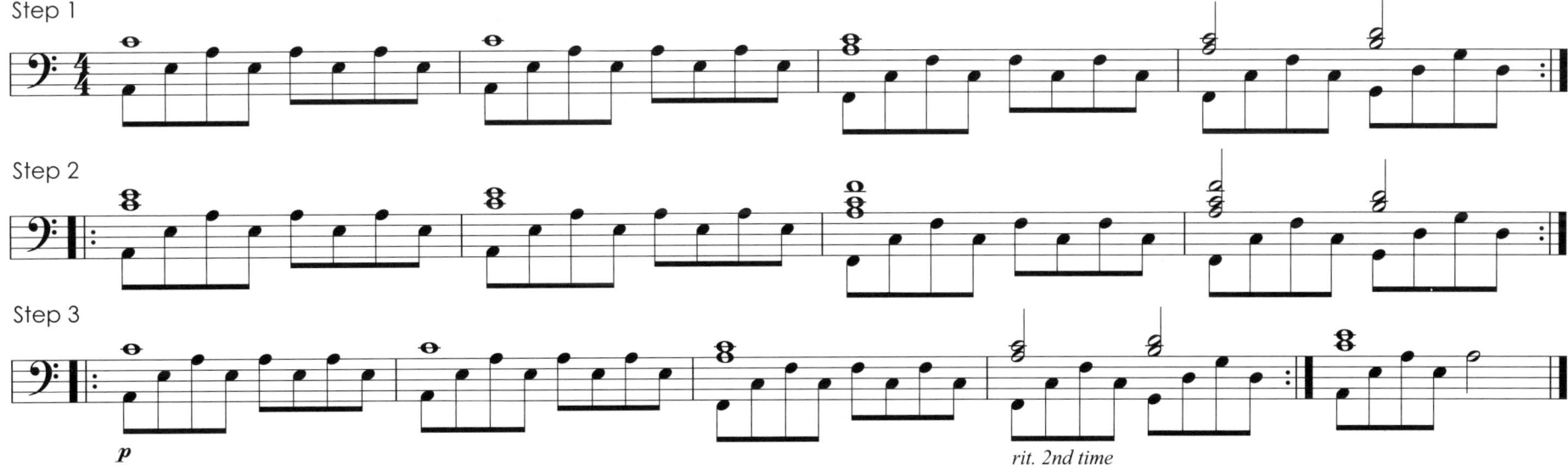

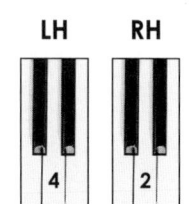

RAINFOREST MYSTERY

Andante

Hague

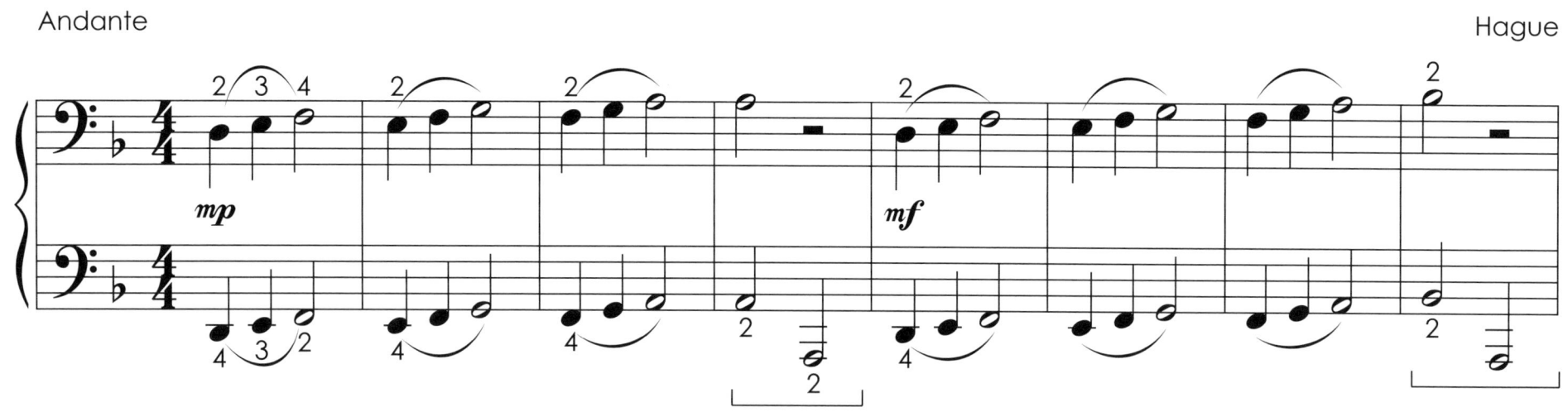
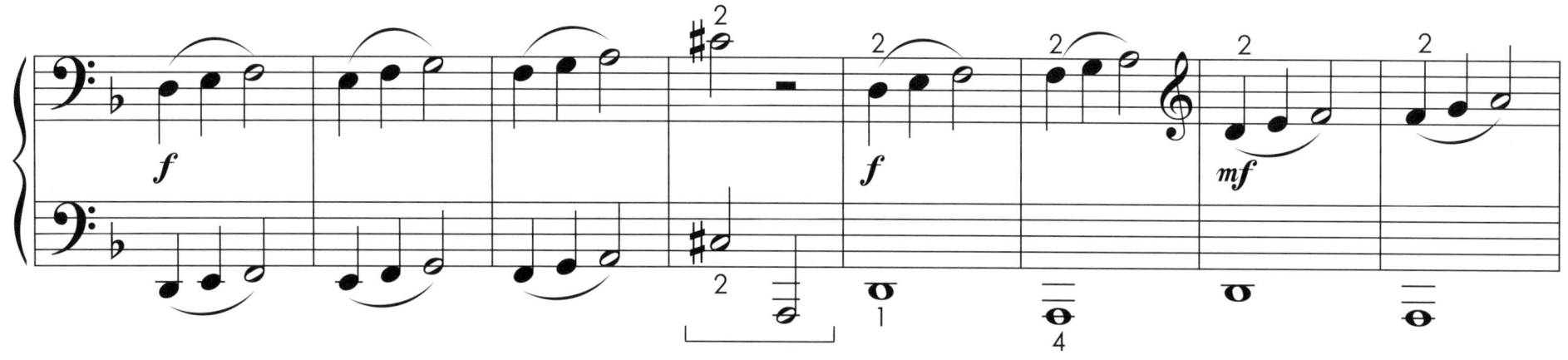

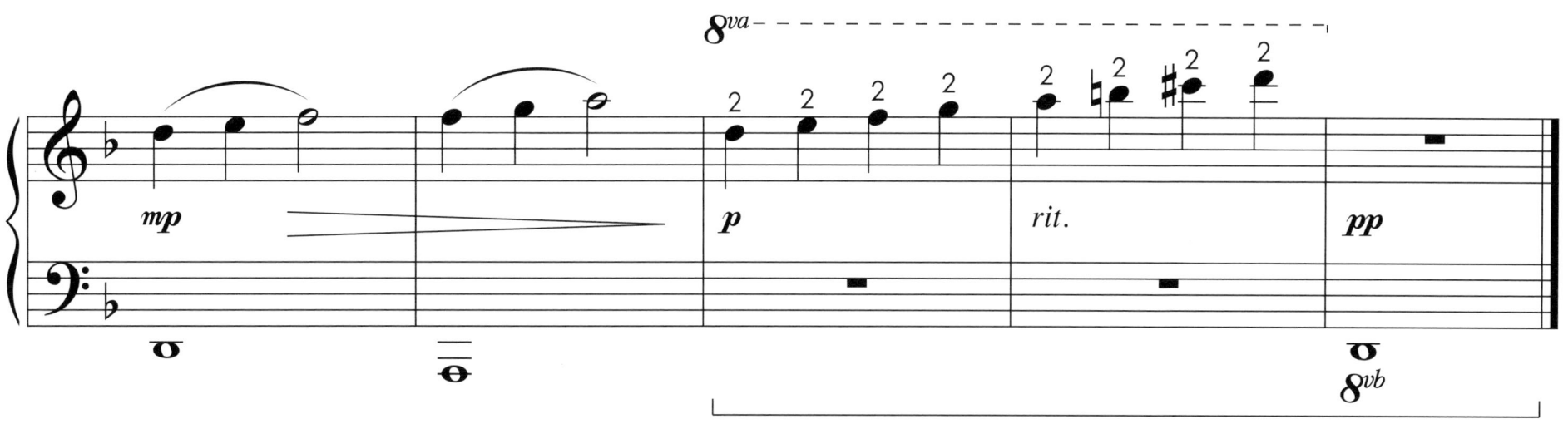

PING PONG

UNIT 4
READING

Allegro

Hague

Play - ing ping pong with my broth - er. Play - ing ping pong with my sis - ter.

5

Play - ing ping pong af - ter school is what we like to do!

5

What three notes do you play in this piece? _____ _____ _____

Crazy Ping Pong Variation: Assign one note name to yourself and one note each to two of your friends. As you and your friends play the piece, play your assigned note in any octave.

Challenge: Play Hands Together in parallel motion.

Teacher Accompaniment

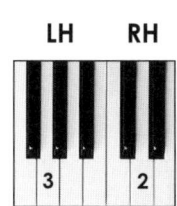

BAA, BAA, BLACK SHEEP

English Folk Song, arr. Hague

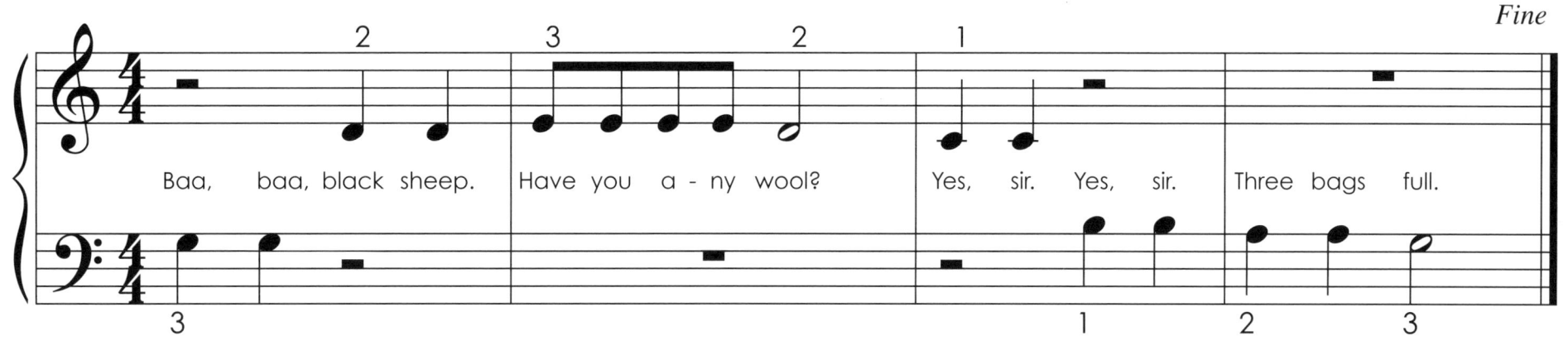
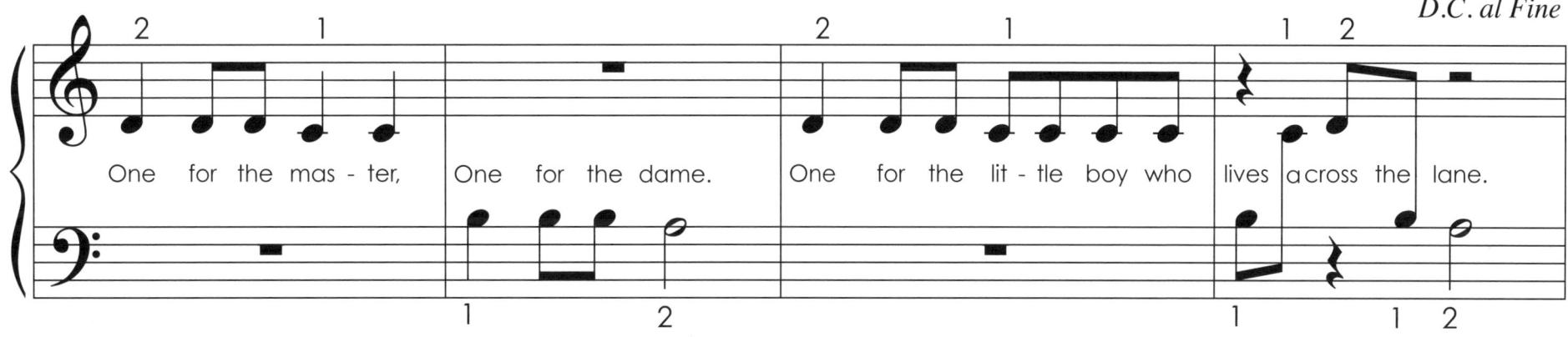

Teacher Accompaniment. Student plays one octave higher than written.

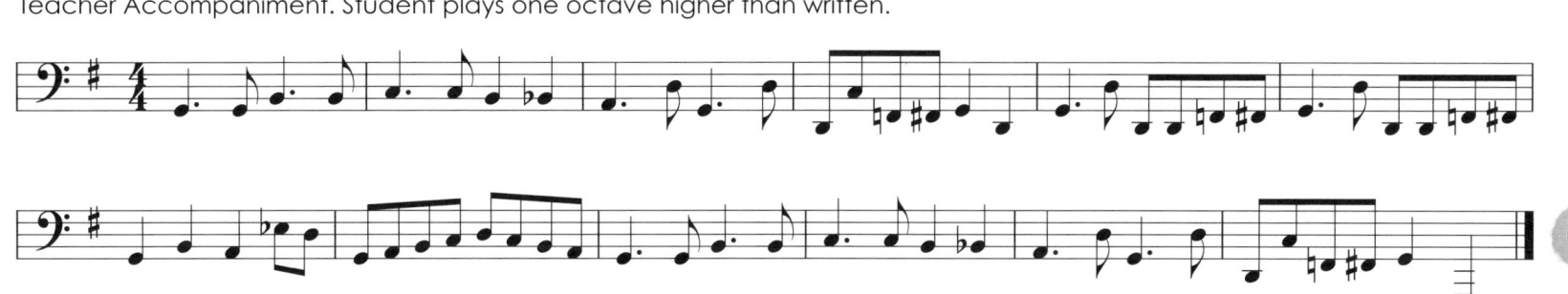

AUTUMN

UNIT 4
READING

Moderato

Hague & Fisher

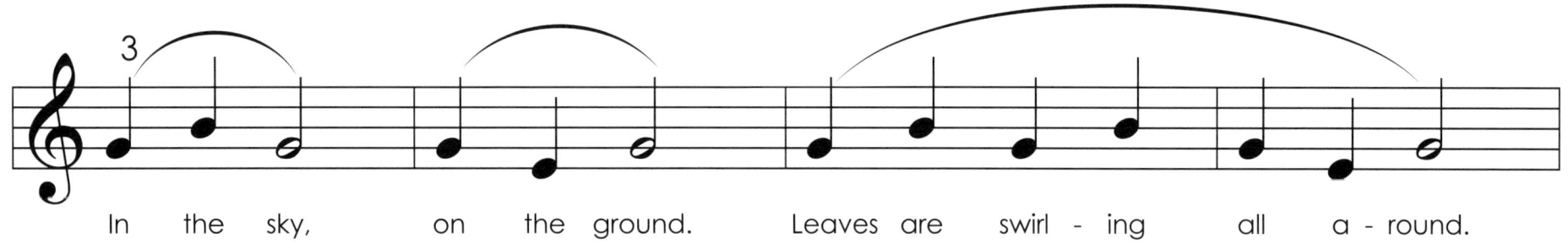

In the sky, on the ground. Leaves are swirl - ing all a - round.

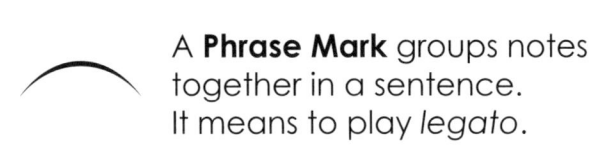

A **Phrase Mark** groups notes together in a sentence. It means to play *legato*.

A **Minim Rest** equals two beats of silence. When you count it, whisper "Rest - 2."

Teacher Accompaniment

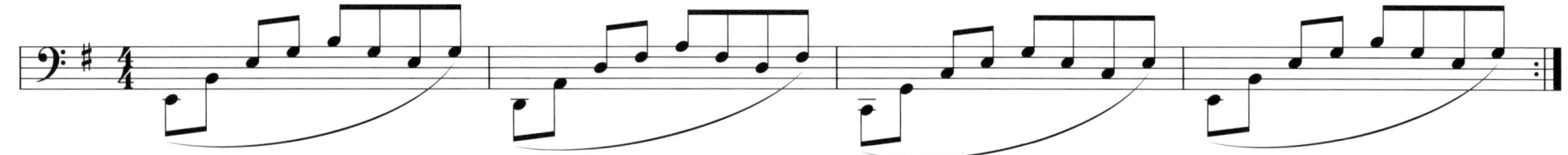

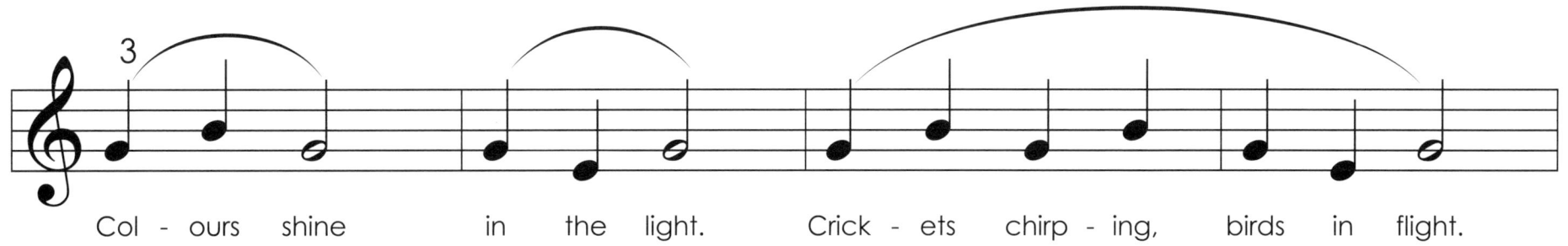
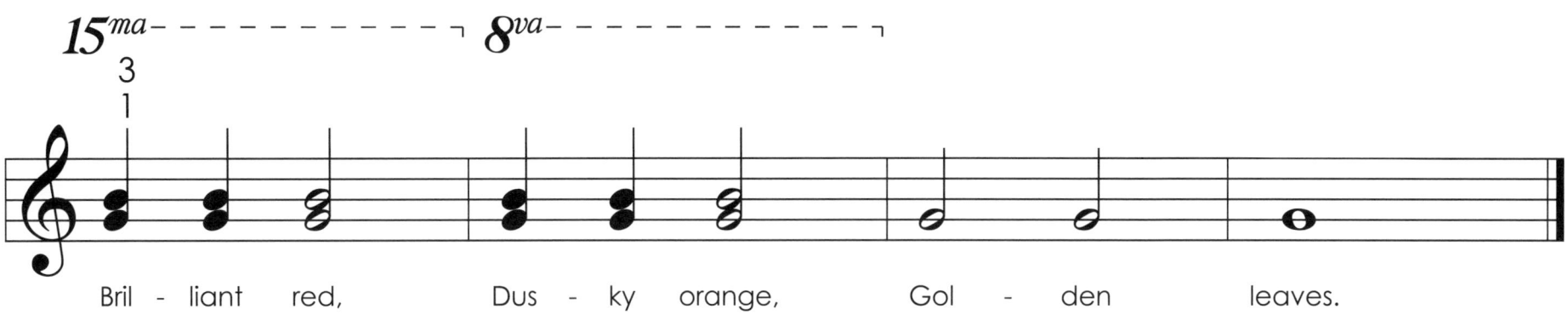

KANGAROO
Left Hand

UNIT 4
TECHNIQUE

Hague

DO YOU HAVE?

- Small bounces on "Kanga" and a larger bounce on "roo."
- Firm fingertips
- Loose wrist

Teacher Accompaniment

KANGAROO
Right Hand

UNIT 4
TECHNIQUE

Hague

Kan - ga - roo

Teacher Accompaniment

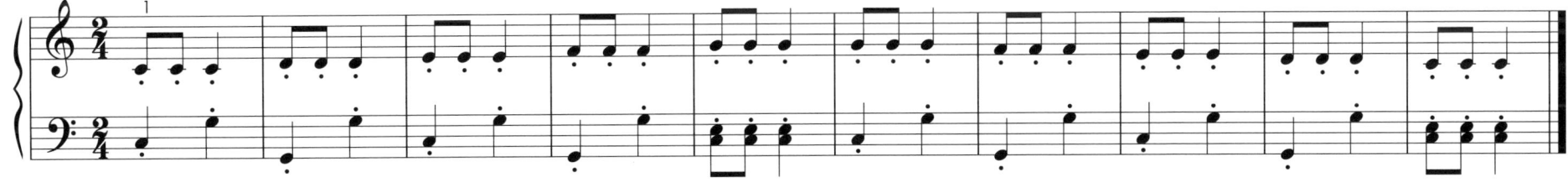

KANGAROO TAKES A TRIP

Step 1 Learn this Kangaroo Pattern with the RH.

Step 2

Write Finger Numbers in the boxes. The first two have been completed for you to match the Kangaroo Pattern above.

Next, play with the accompaniment in the order of the fingers you have selected below.

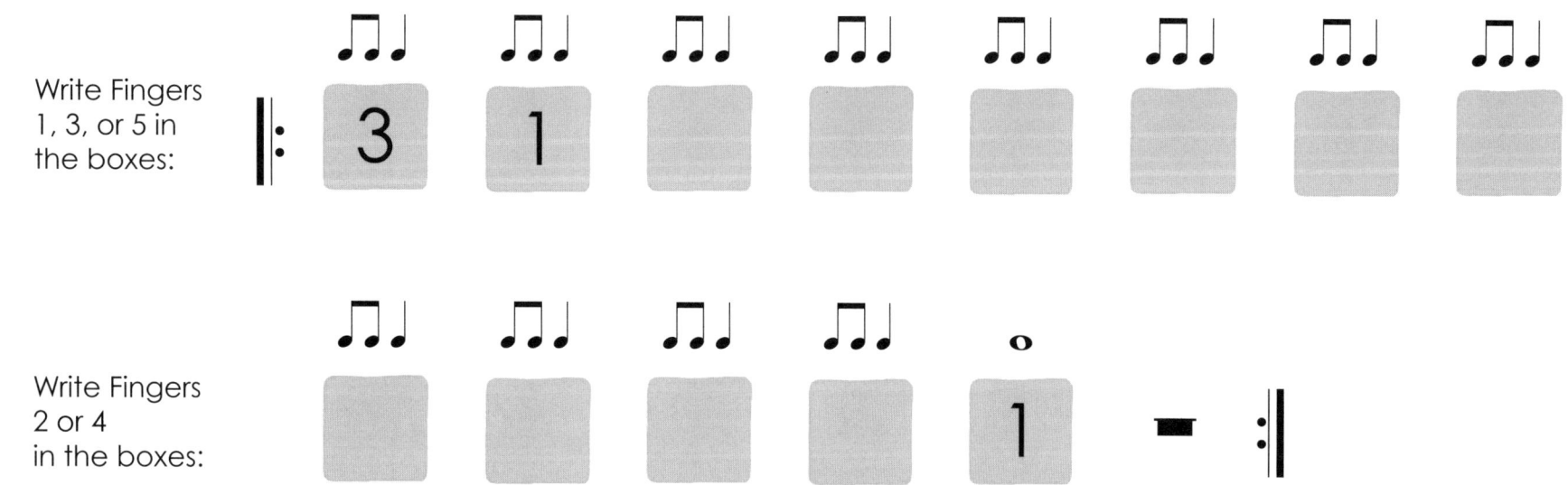

TRY THIS!

- Play the finger numbers with the LH instead of the RH.
- Play in a high octave or a low octave.
- Write finger numbers in a different colour under the boxes to create a new improvisation.
- Play at a slow tempo, like a tired kangaroo, or a fast tempo, like an excited kangaroo.

Teacher Accompaniment

Hague

KRISTABEL KANGAROO VISITS KOREA

Allegro

Hague

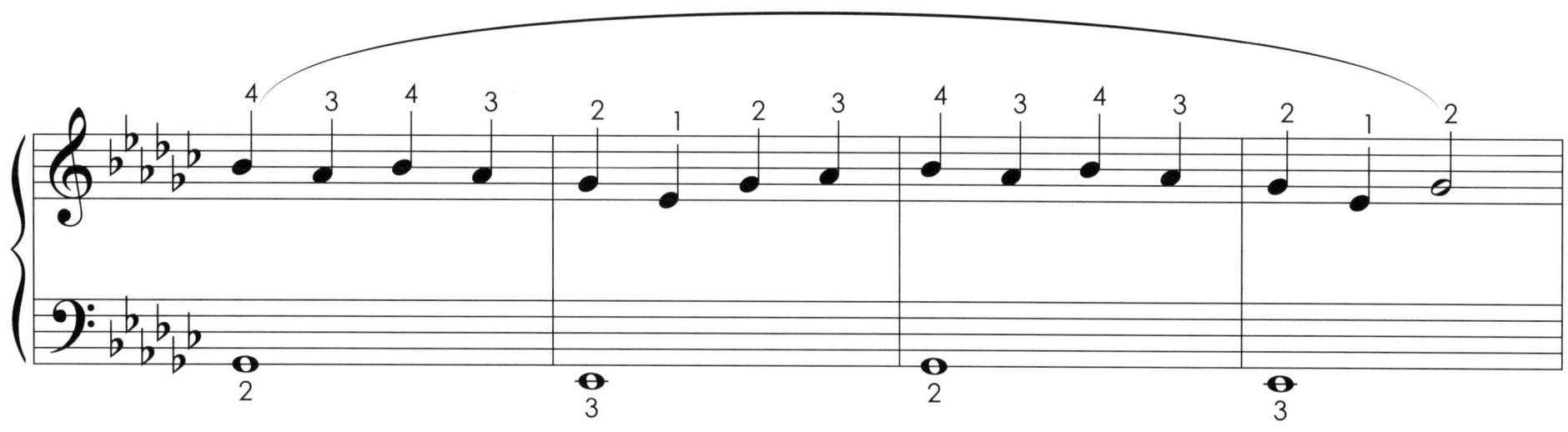

MATTHEW MONKEY

Moderato
Hague & Fisher

UNIT 4
READING

Mat - thew Mon - key is a play - ful guy!

Mat - thew Mon - key swings from trees, shakes a branch and drops some leaves.
Hides in - side the big leaf pile, jumps out fast and gives a smile!

Teacher Accompaniment

104

THE HIPPOPOTAMUS AND THE MOSQUITO

UNIT 4
READING

Andante

Fisher

f **forte** means to play loudly.

CHALLENGE!

Play Hands Together in parallel motion. Begin with RH Finger 3 on C one octave above the LH.

Teacher Accompaniment

2NDS AND 3RDS

UNIT 5
THEORY

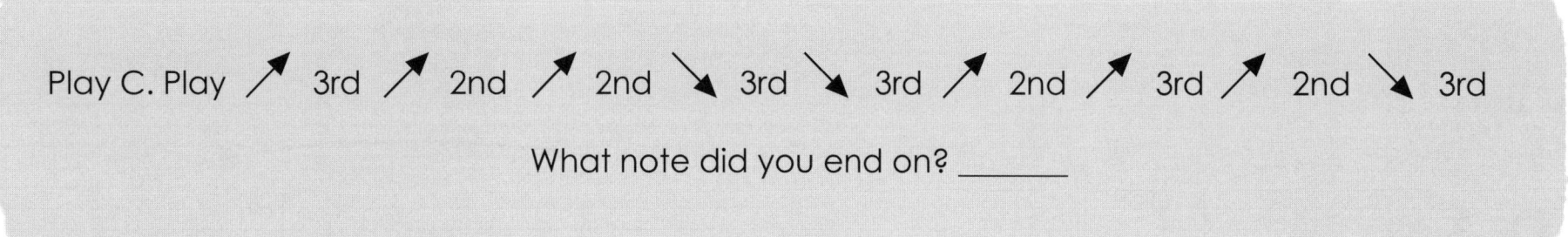

What note did you end on? _____

Circle the bars with 2nds. Put a box around the bars with 3rds.

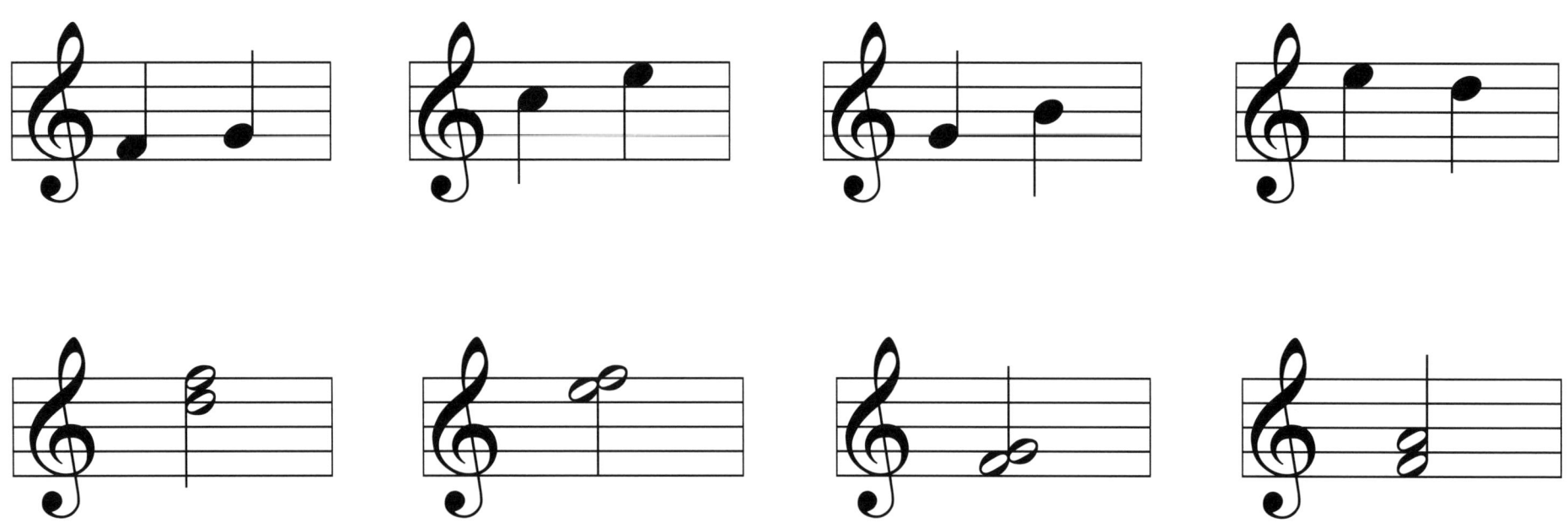

Assign Piano Safari Sight Reading & Rhythm Cards Level E during Unit 5.

EARL THE SQUIRREL

UNIT 5
READING

Moderato

Hague & Stevens

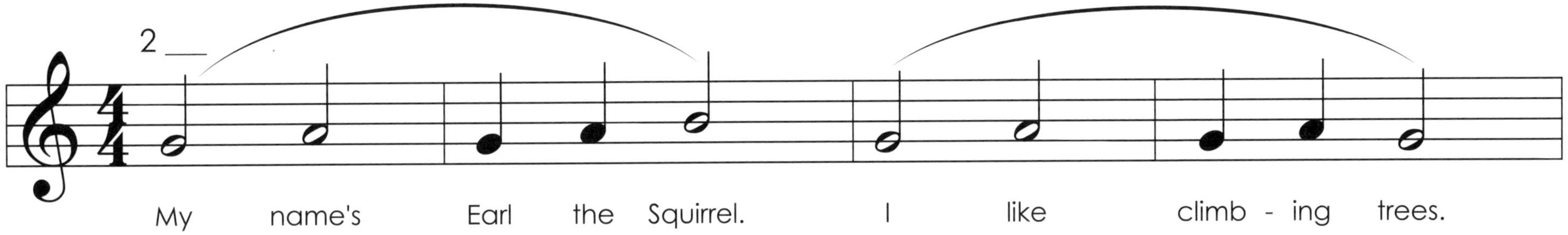
2
My name's Earl the Squirrel. I like climb - ing trees.

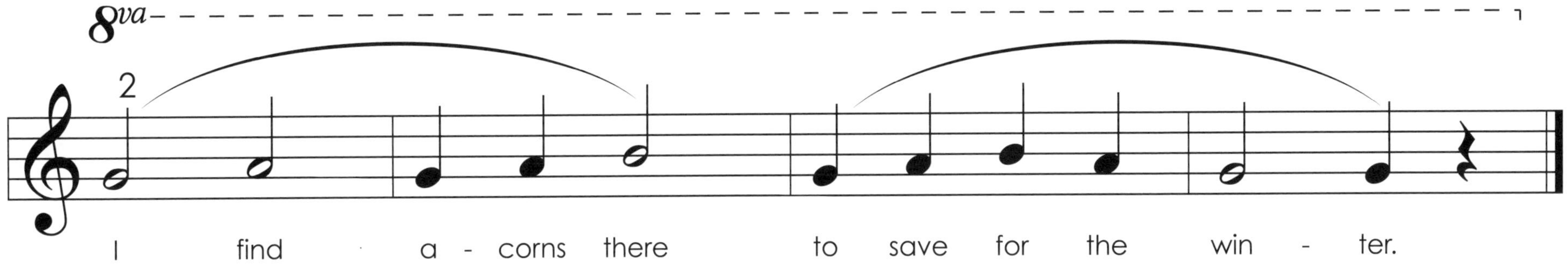
8va
2
I find a - corns there to save for the win - ter.

Teacher Accompaniment

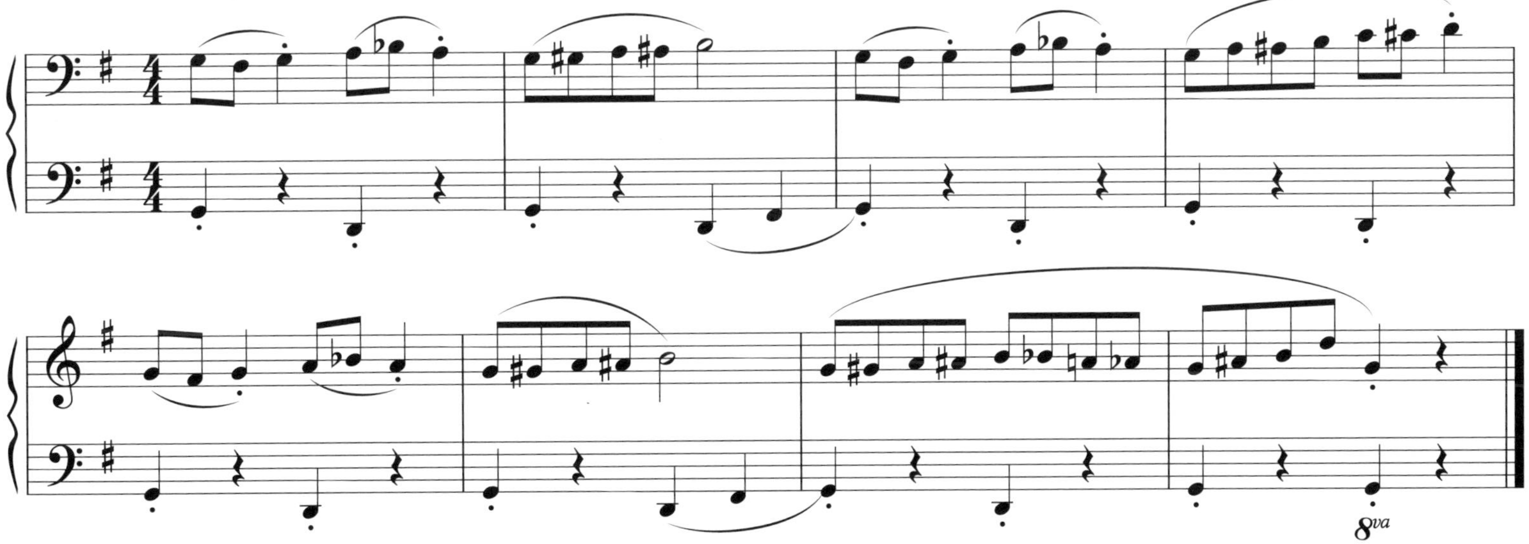
8va

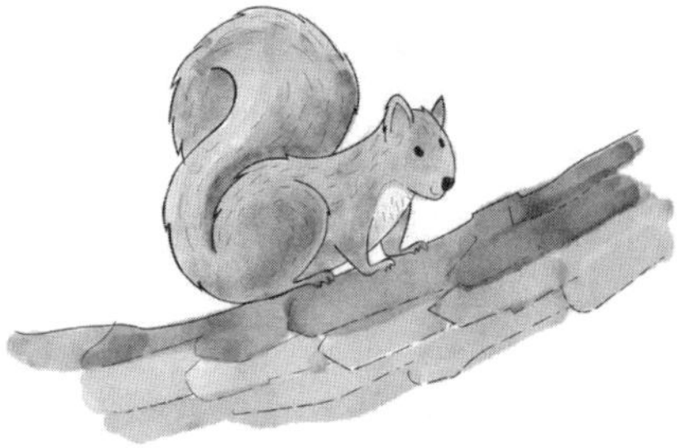

WHALE IN THE DEEP

UNIT 5
READING

Andante

Fisher

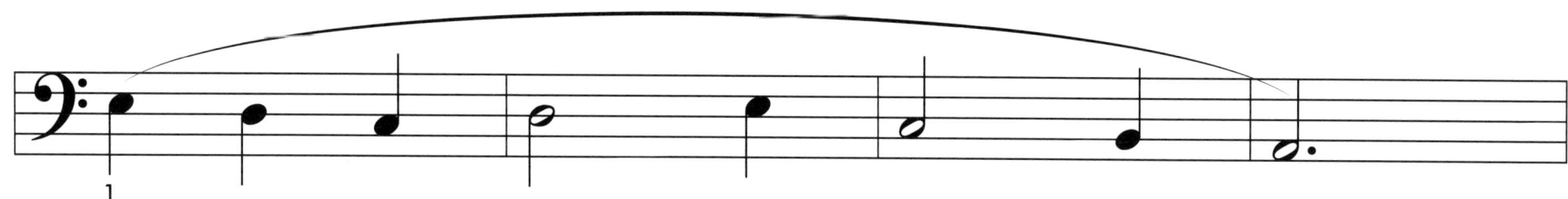

mp *mezzo piano* means to play medium quiet.

Teacher Accompaniment. Student plays one octave higher than written.

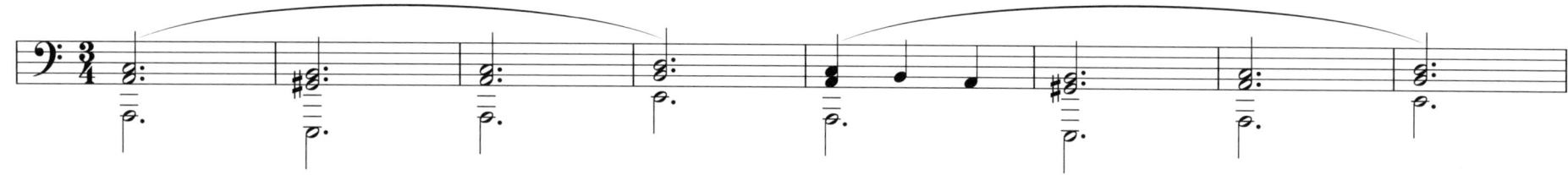

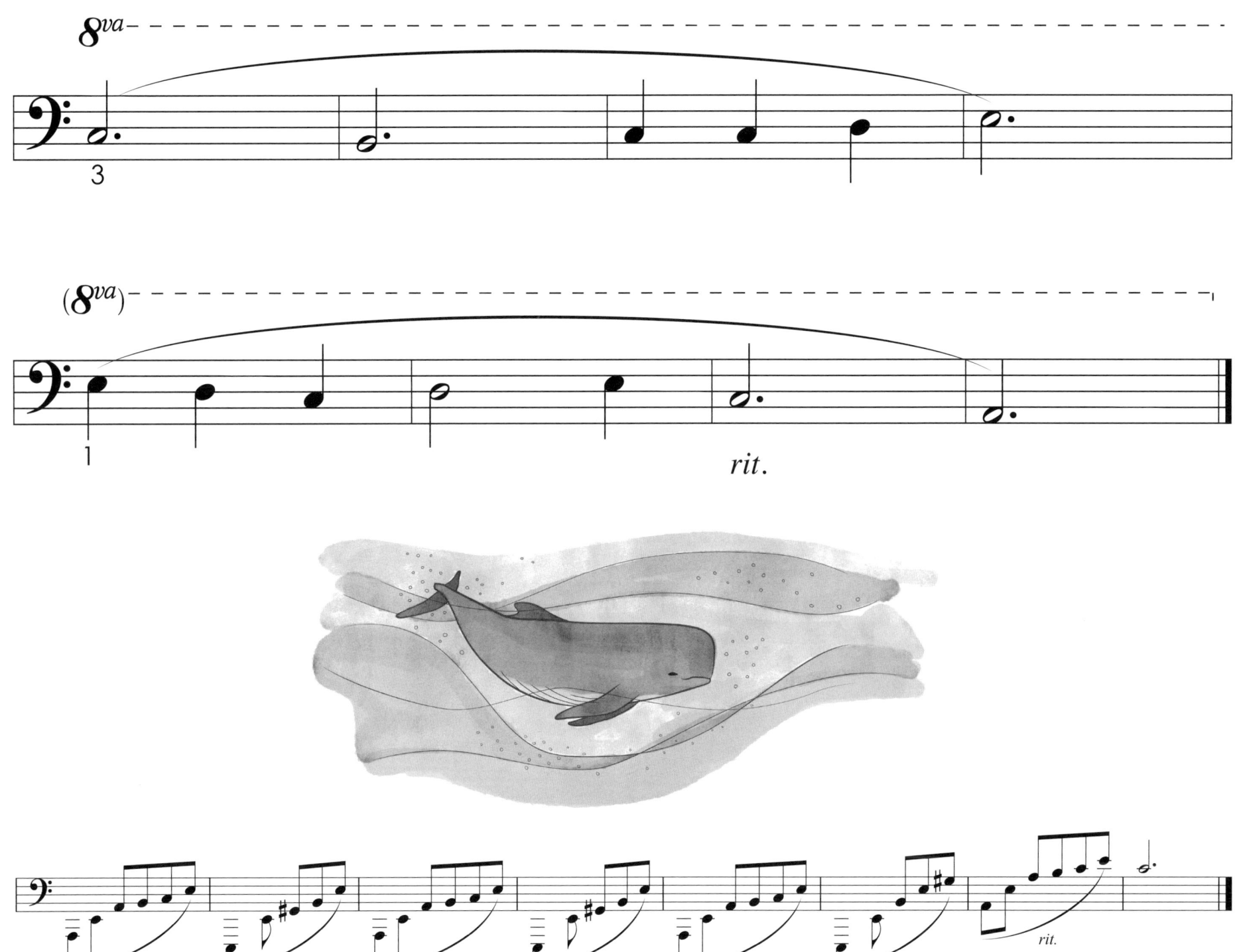

SOARING BIRD
Left Hand

UNIT 5
TECHNIQUE

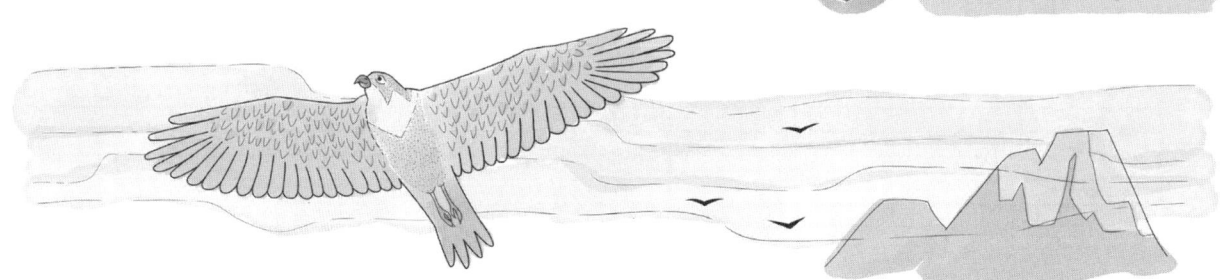

Hague

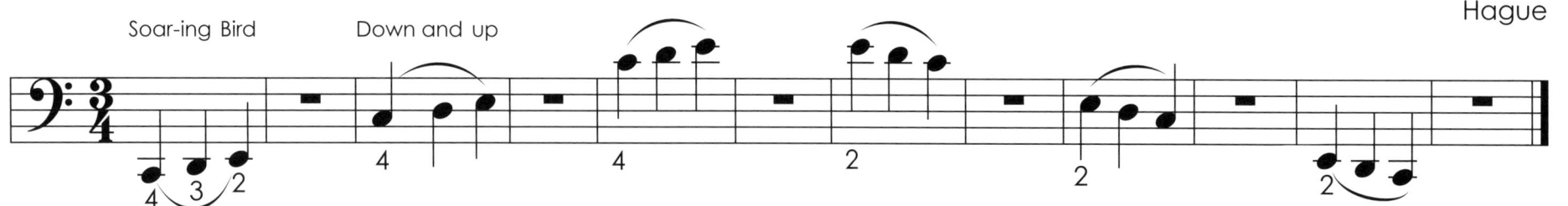

DO YOU HAVE?

- Smooth down-up motion of the arm
- Graceful arch to new position
- *Legato* sound

Teacher Accompaniment

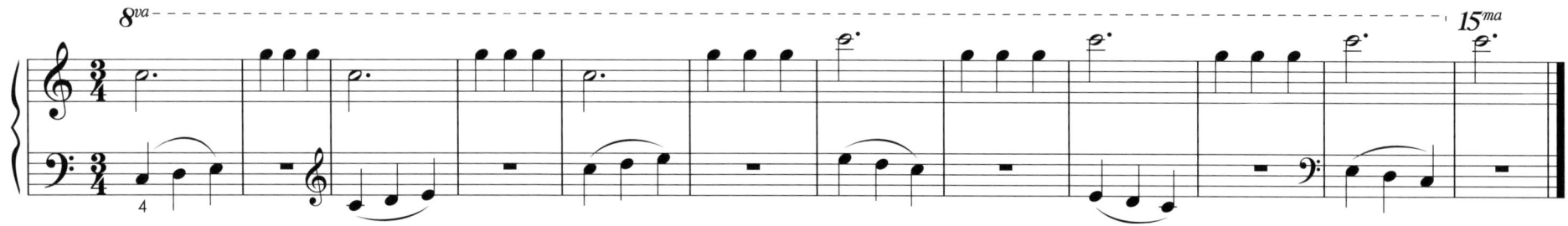

SOARING BIRD
Right Hand

UNIT 5
TECHNIQUE

Hague

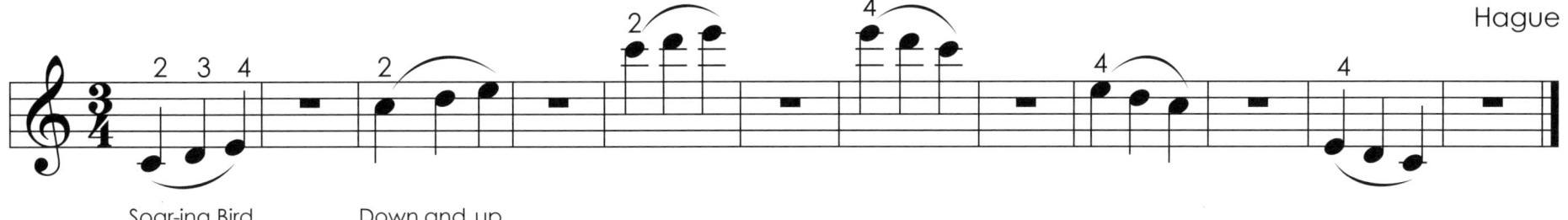

Soar-ing Bird   Down and up

Draw a line to match each definition with the correct animal:

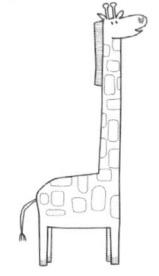

Non legato with an arm bounce on each note

Legato with a smooth arm motion for the whole phrase

Legato fingers combined with a bouncy arm

Teacher Accompaniment

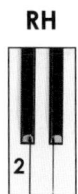

WHITE BIRD, BLACK BIRD

UNIT 5
IMPROVISATION

Step 1

Learn this Bird Pattern with RH.

Hague & Fisher

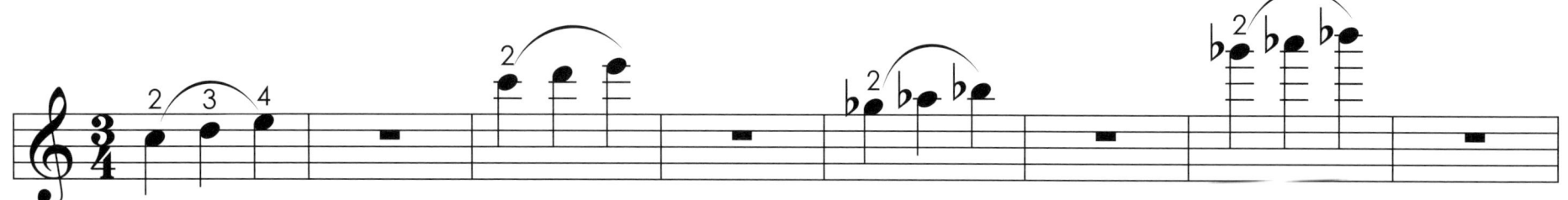

Step 2

As your teacher plays the accompaniment, play the Bird Pattern, and then continue playing with Soaring Bird Technique, alternating two groups of white keys with two groups of black keys.

Step 3

In the middle of your improvisation, speed up the tempo as your bird swoops and dives over the mountain peaks. Near the end of the piece, slow down as your bird prepares to land.

Step 4 Draw a picture that describes the music you create.

TRY THIS!

- Play in different octaves
- Play patterns going up and down
- Change the order of the notes. For example, play 2 4 3 instead of 2 3 4.
- Use LH instead of RH
- Change the dynamics
- Hands together in parallel motion

Teacher Accompaniment   Repeat as many times as desired.

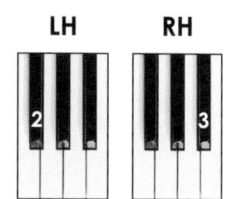

HAWK ON THE MOUNTAIN PEAK

UNIT 5
ROTE

The hawk sits proudly on a craggy peak…

Hague & Fisher

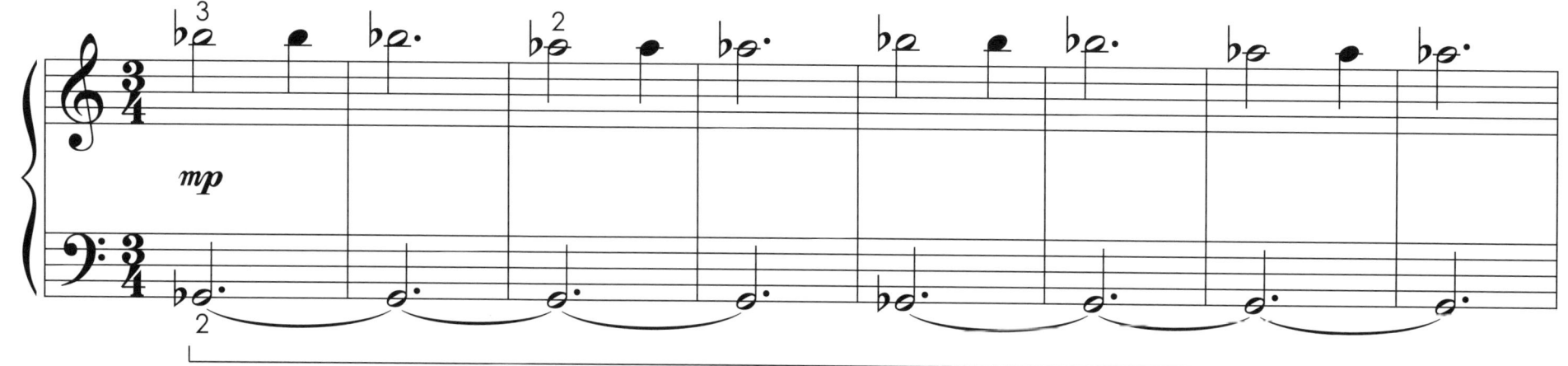

He opens his wings and soars upward into the leaden sky…

After a lazy circle, he swoops down and skims the treetops...

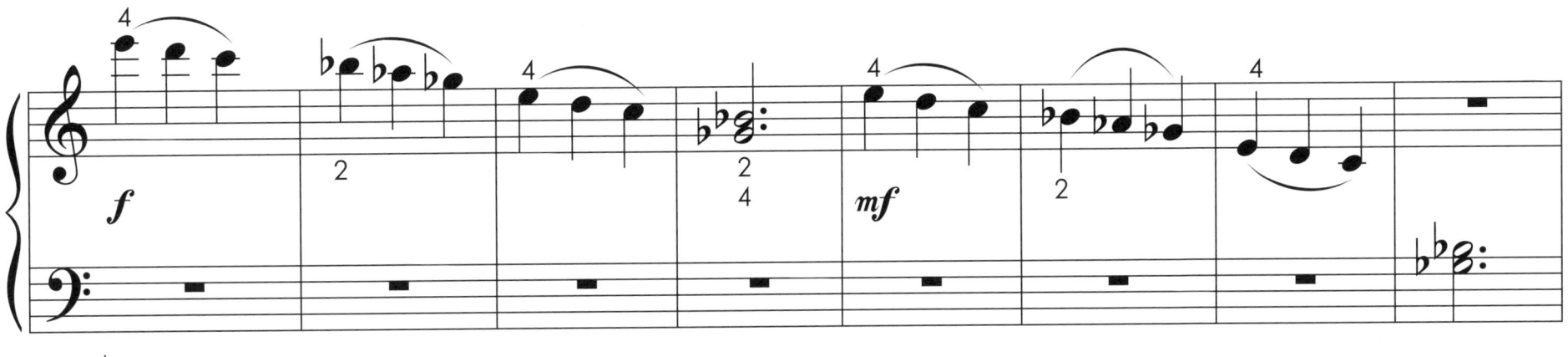

Returning to his watchful perch.

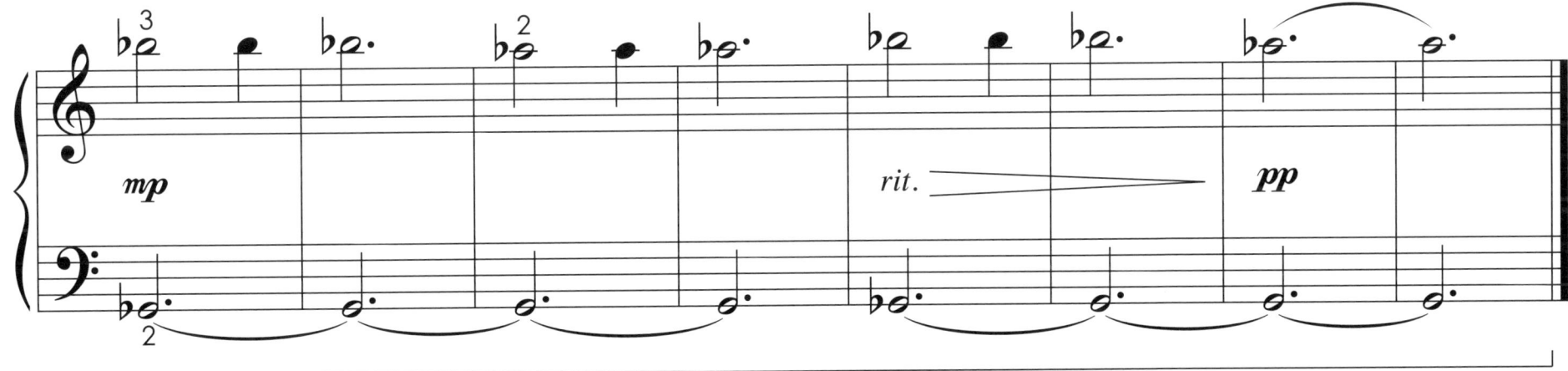

115

BLUEBIRD, BLUEBIRD

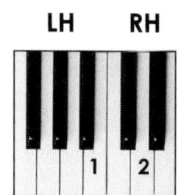

UNIT 5
FOLK

Moderato

American Folk Song, arr. Hague

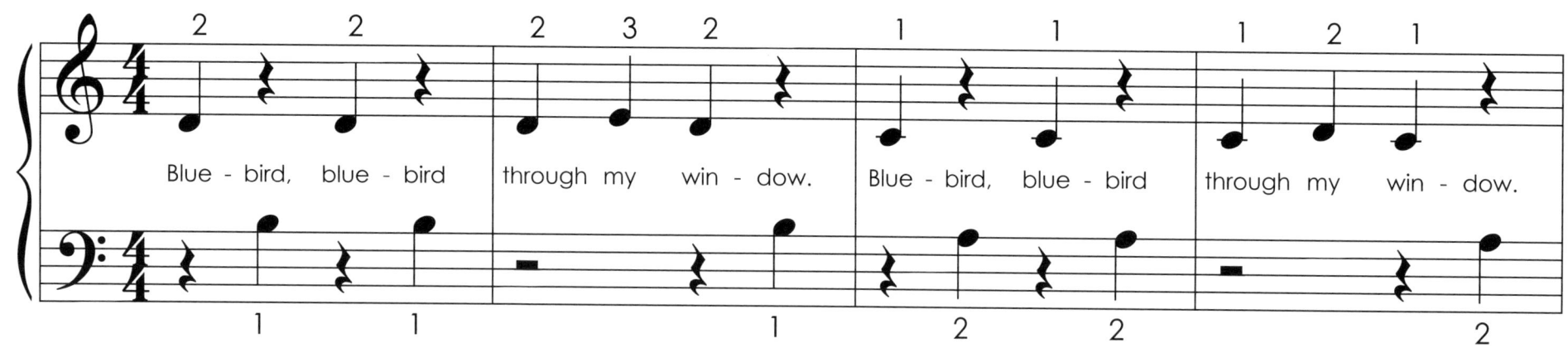
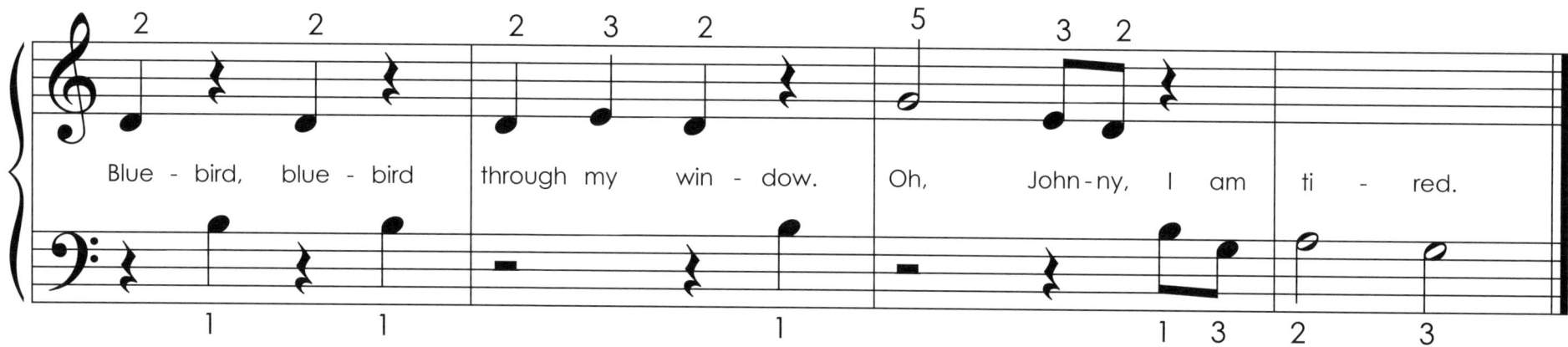

Teacher Accompaniment. Student plays one octave higher than written.

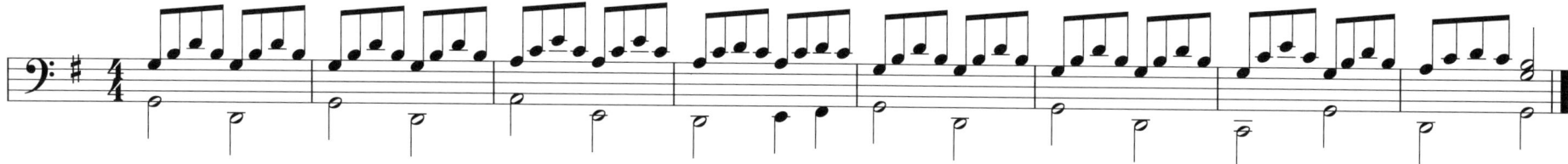

TWELVE BAR BLUES

UNIT 5 IMPROVISATION

Student Part:

- Put page marking tabs or stickers on the keys the student will play.
- The student improvises on the notes of the Blues Scale by playing the marked keys using RH, LH, or both hands. The student may use Finger 2 or a fingering of the teacher's choice.

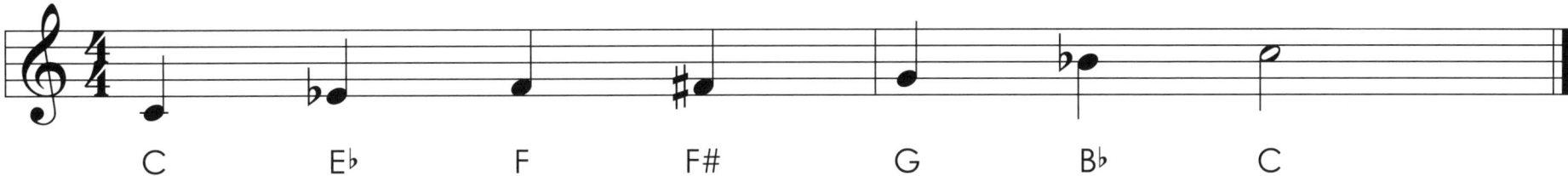

C E♭ F F# G B♭ C

Teacher Part:

- The teacher plays the following accompaniment while the student improvises. Swing the quavers.
- Vary the accompaniment as desired.

Hague

Introduction   1 2 Ready Play

117

THE MOSQUITO AND THE HIPPOPOTAMUS

UNIT 5
READING

Allegro

Fisher & Hague

The Mosquito dances around the Hippopotamus.

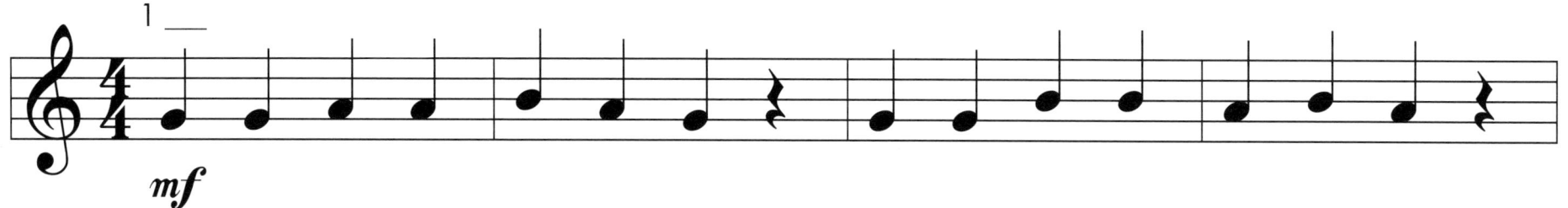

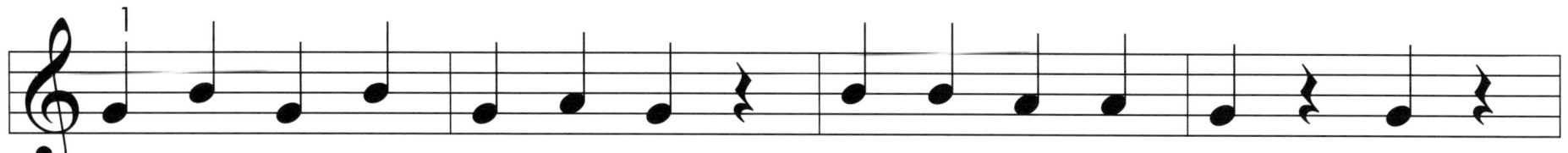

Teacher Accompaniment

Both hands one octave lower than written.

The Mosquito flies up for the bite!

You may play this piece four ways:

1. **Duet**: You play Right Hand. A friend plays Left Hand.

2. **Duet**: You play Left Hand. A friend plays Right Hand.

3. **Solo**: Play Hands Together!

4. **Dragon Stampede**: Play with as many people on as many pianos as you have available. Can you fit four people on a piano? Six people? Eight people at two pianos?

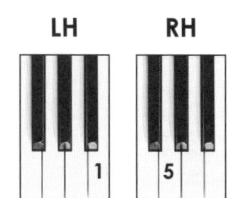

A COWBOY'S LIFE

UNIT 5
FOLK

Moderato

American Folk Song, arr. Hague, lyrics Fisher

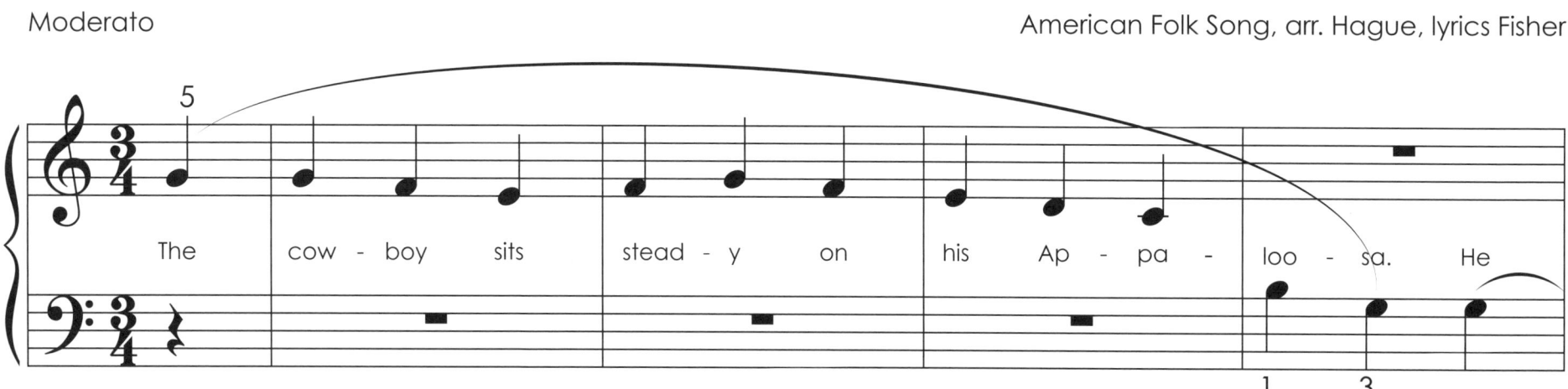

The cow - boy sits stead - y on his Ap - pa - loo - sa. He digs in his spurs and then rides like the wind. He

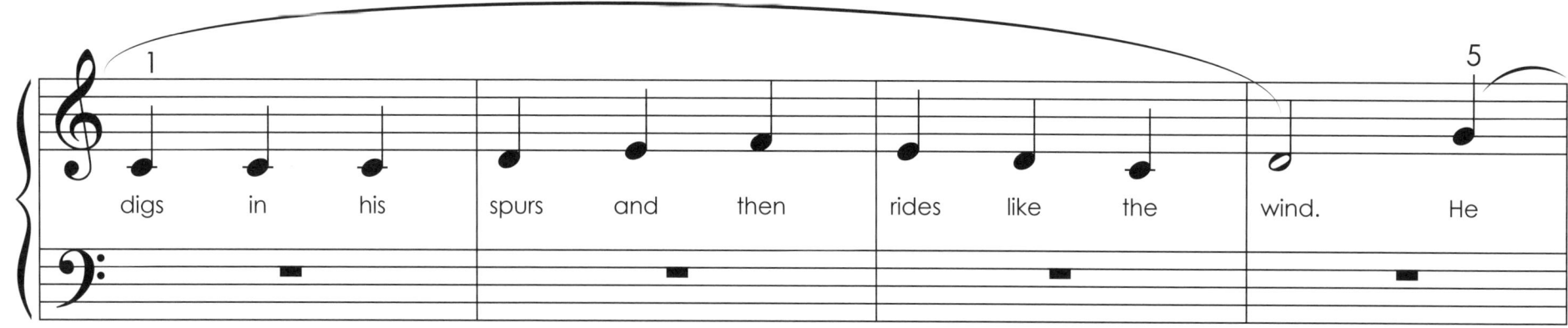

Teacher Accompaniment. Student plays one octave higher than written.

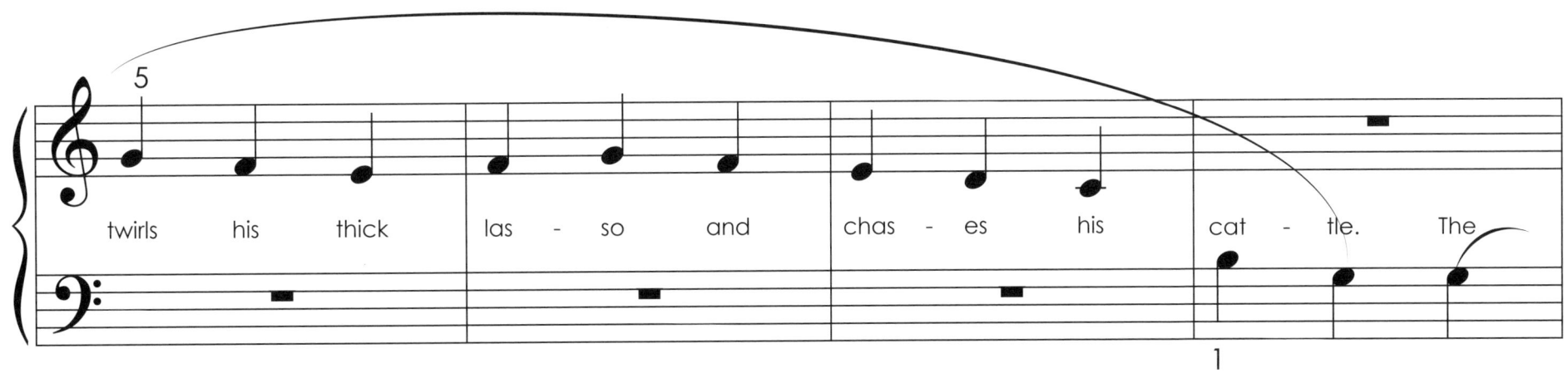
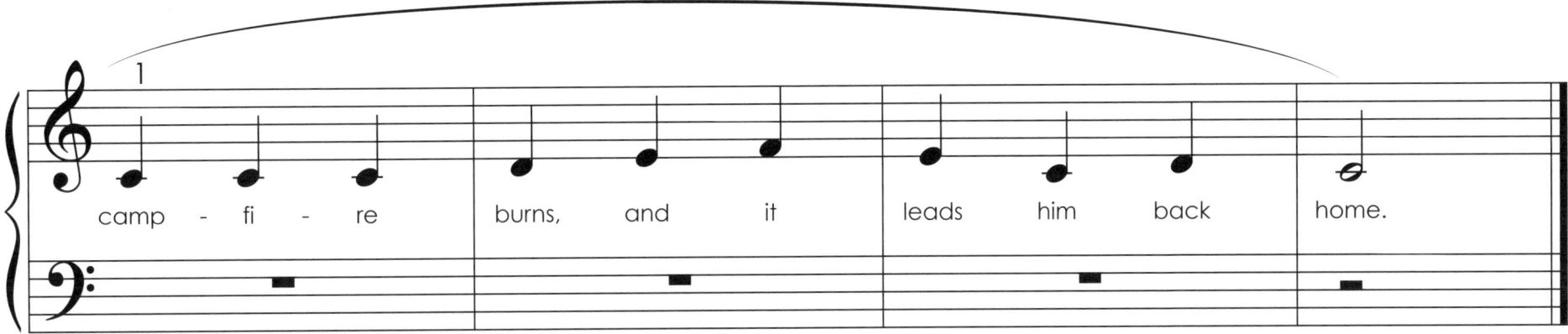
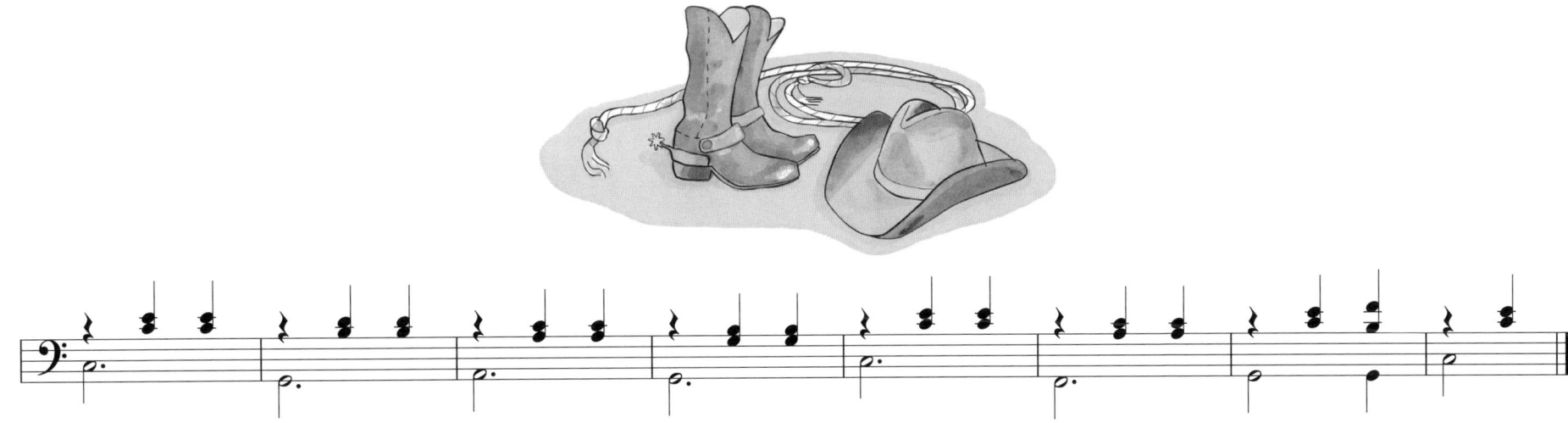

TALENT SHOW

UNIT 5
READING

Moderato

American Folk Song, arr. Fisher & Stevens

Tal - ent show!   Kan - ga - roo   boun - ces high.   Tal - ent show!   Fi - re - flies spin.

Tal - ent show!   Ow - ls screech   in   the   sky.   Tal - ent show!   Who   will   win?

This is a **Slur** mark. It means to play *legato* with a down-up motion.

Teacher Accompaniment

FOREST NIGHT

Andante

Hague & Fisher

UNIT 5
READING

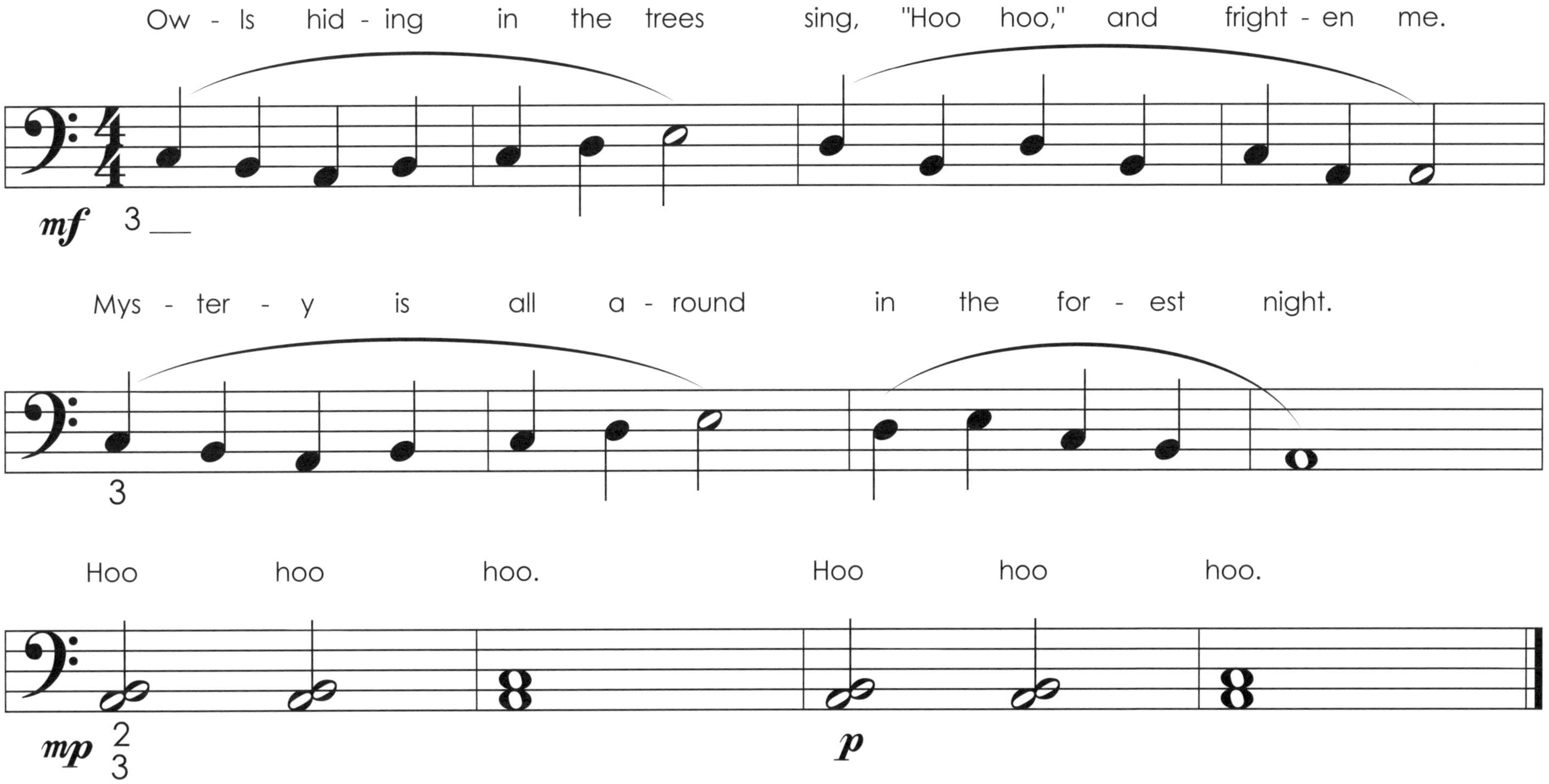

Teacher Accompaniment. Student plays one octave higher than written.

MONKEY SWINGING IN A TREE
Left Hand

UNIT 5
TECHNIQUE

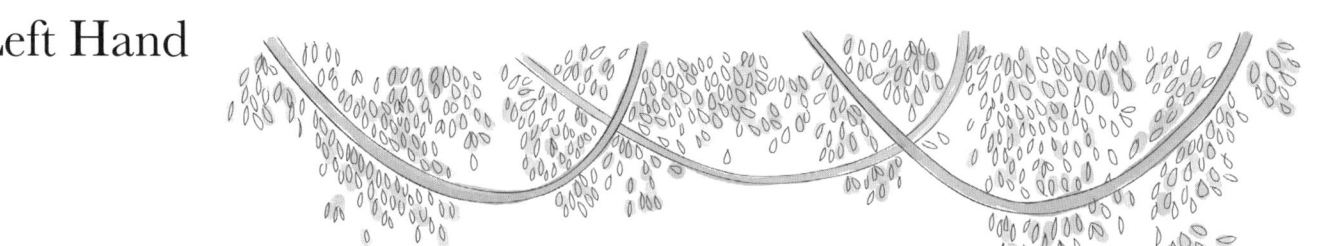

Mon - key swing - ing in a tree.

Hague

DO YOU HAVE?

- Rotation of the forearm, transferring arm weight from finger to finger to produce a *legato* sound
- Hand up over the keys
- Strong fingertips
- Relaxed thumb

Teacher Accompaniment

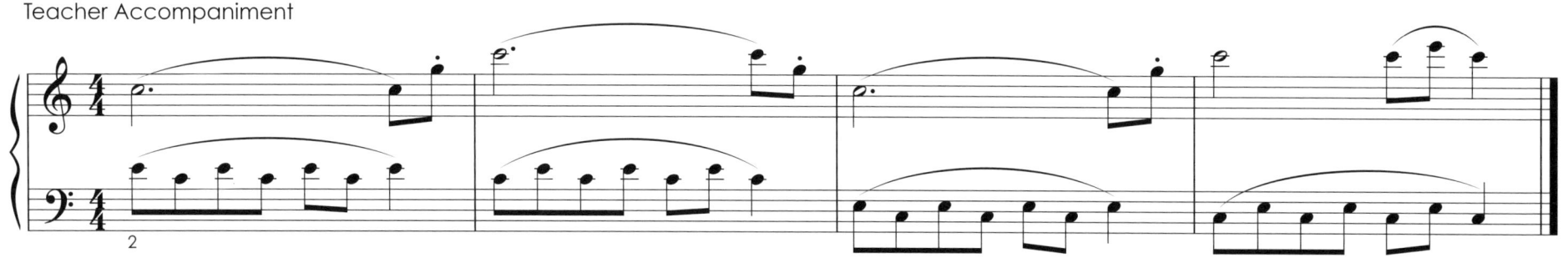

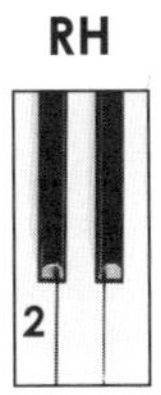

MONKEY SWINGING IN A TREE
Right Hand

UNIT 5
TECHNIQUE

Hague

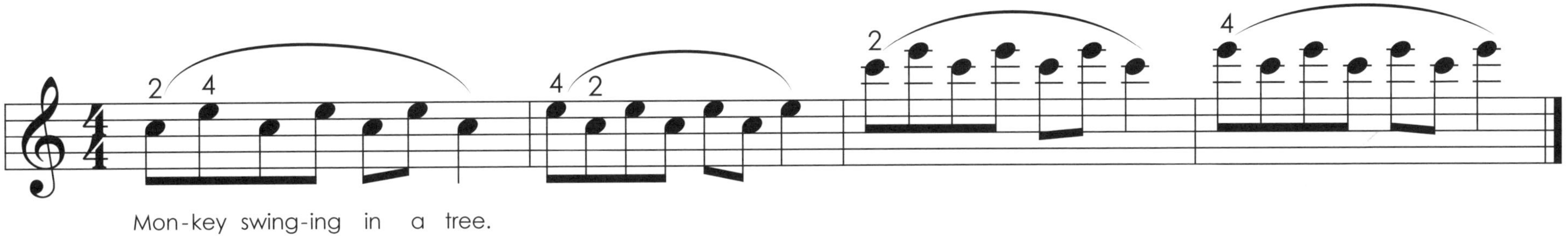

Mon-key swing-ing in a tree.

Teacher Accompaniment

JUNGLE JUMPS

UNIT 5
IMPROVISATION

Step 1

Play the Monkey Pattern starting with RH Finger 2 on C.

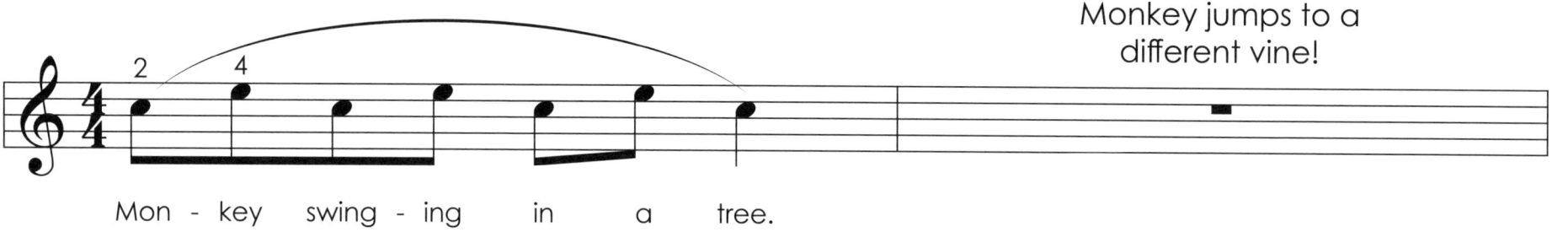

Monkey jumps to a different vine!

Mon - key swing - ing in a tree.

Step 2

During the rest in bar 2 above, quickly move Finger 2 to a different white key. Play the Monkey Pattern beginning on the white key you have chosen.

Step 3

Continue playing the Monkey Pattern on different white keys while your teacher plays the accompaniment.

Step 4

Signal the end of your improvisation by playing the Monkey Pattern beginning with Finger 2 on C and slowing down.

TRY THIS!

- Use Fingers 1 and 3
- Use LH instead of RH
- Play Hands Together
- Play slow or fast

Teacher Accompaniment

Step 1:

Hague

Steps 2 - 3:

As the student moves to a different white key with Finger 2, transpose the pattern above to the key the student chooses. Use white keys only. For example, if the student places Finger 2 on A, play the pattern above in A Minor.

Step 4: End in C.

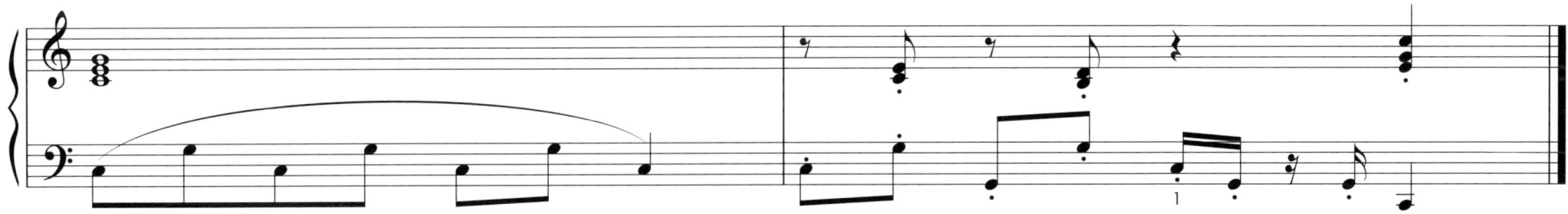

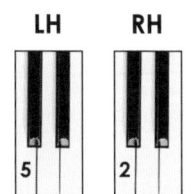

MONKEY BLUES

Allegro

Hague

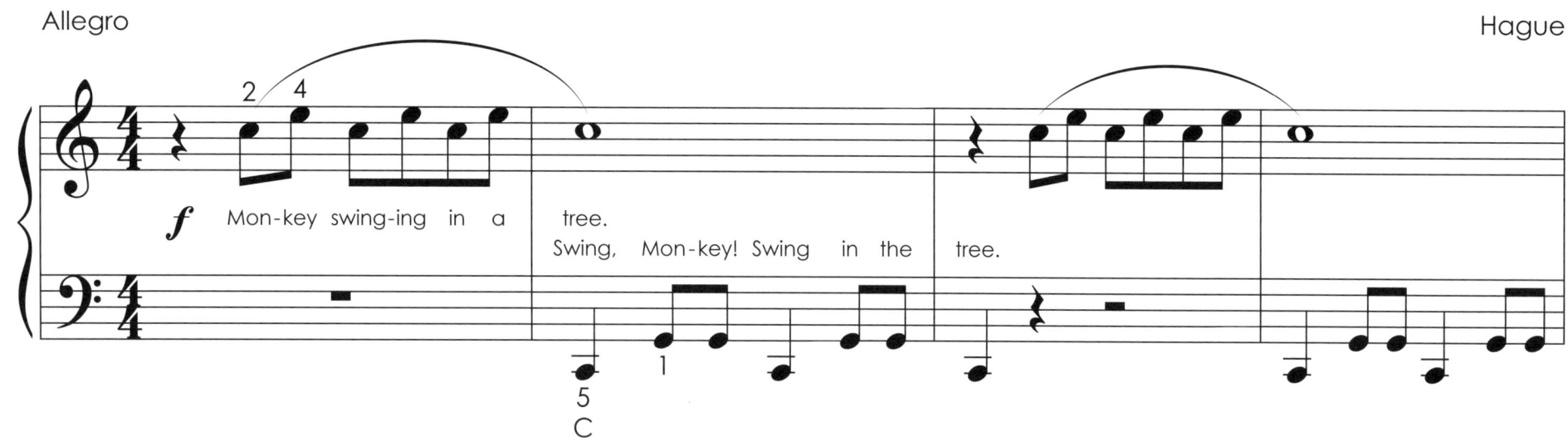

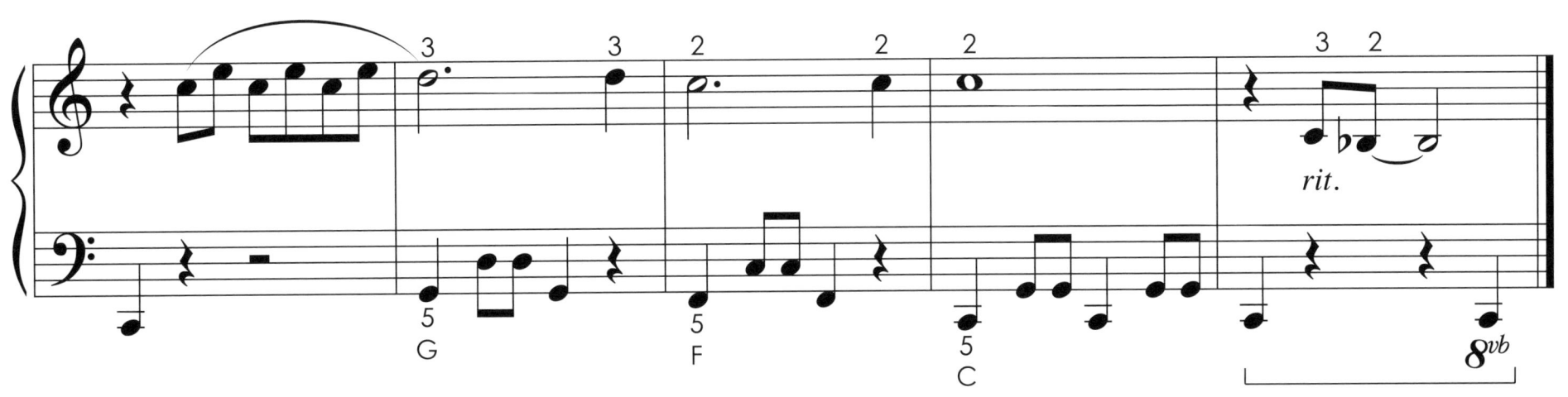
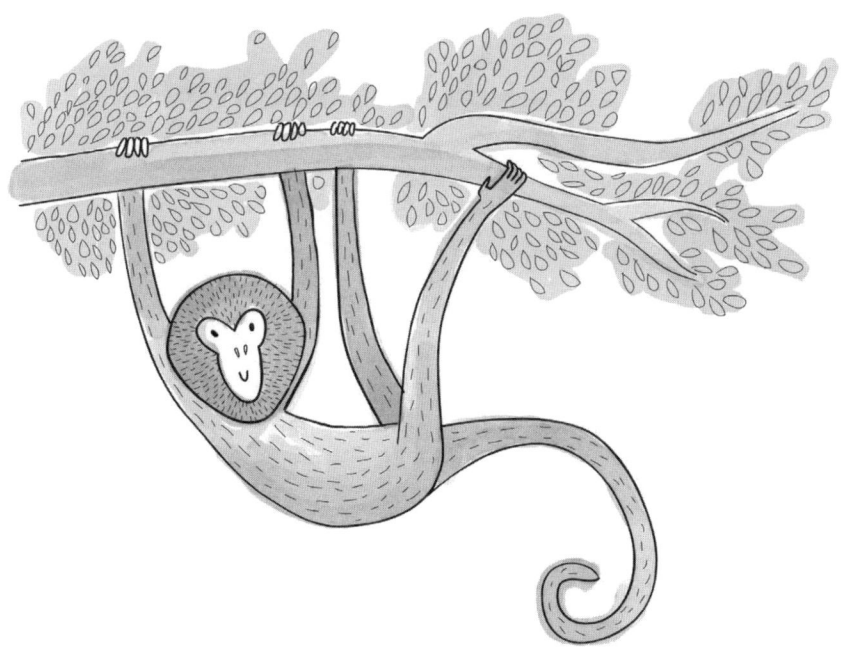

131

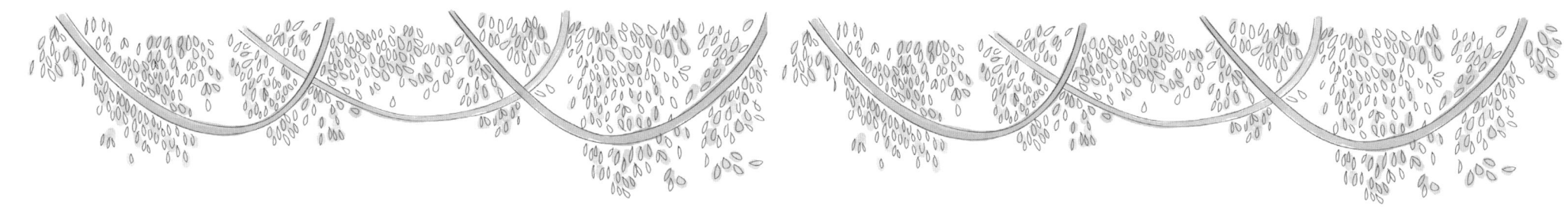

CONGRATULATIONS!

YOU HAVE COMPLETED PIANO SAFARI REPERTOIRE BOOK 1

AND ARE PROMOTED TO PIANO SAFARI REPERTOIRE BOOK 2

_____

Teacher Signature

_____

Date

ABOUT THE AUTHORS

KATHERINE FISHER is on the faculty of Ohio University in Athens, Ohio. Her responsibilities include teaching piano pedagogy and applied piano as well as coordinating the Piano Safari Program (group lessons) for children who are beginners at the instrument.

Katherine Fisher and Dr. Julie Knerr Hague developed the Piano Safari® Method during their time in school together at the University of Oklahoma. While graduate students, they realised they had a mutual dream of writing a piano method that would incorporate the best elements of the various techniques they had been using in their teaching.

Katherine, a Yamaha artist, is a member of the Fisher Piano Duo with husband, Dr. Christopher Fisher. The duo has performed throughout the United States. They are co-authors of the revised and expanded edition of *Piano Duet Repertoire* (Indiana University Press, 2016).

A native of Ohio, Katherine received her degrees from the University of Oklahoma (MM in Piano Performance and Pedagogy) and the Wheaton College Conservatory of Music (BM in Piano Performance). Her former teachers include Jeongwon Ham, Jane Magrath, Barbara Fast, Karin R. Edwards, and Nancy Bachus.

DR. JULIE KNERR HAGUE teaches piano at her home studio in Connecticut.

Julie taught applied piano, piano pedagogy, and group piano as a faculty member at the University of Missouri, Oklahoma City University, Ohio University, and the Hartt School Community Division.

Julie holds a PhD in Music Education with an emphasis in Piano Pedagogy from the University of Oklahoma, where her dissertation on elementary level piano technique was nominated for the Best PhD Dissertation Award in 2006. Additional degrees include MM degrees in Piano Performance and Piano Pedagogy from the University of Illinois at Urbana-Champaign and a BM in Piano Performance from the University of Puget Sound. Her mentors in piano pedagogy include Jane Magrath, Barbara Fast, Christos Tsitsaros, and Reid Alexander.

As an accomplished collaborative pianist, Julie enjoys performing with both instrumentalists and singers. Her former piano teachers include Duane Hulbert, James Barbagallo, William Heiles, Timothy Ehlen, and Edward Gates.

Julie is a frequent lecturer and adjudicator at festivals throughout the United States. Her current research interests include elementary level piano technique, lesser known pre-college piano repertoire, and group piano pedagogy.